Erthe upon Erthe

EARLY ENGLISH TEXT SOCIETY

Original Series, No. 141

1911 (reprinted 1964)

PRICE 30s.

Ne say euer men qui sieut bien ne lehom ne conust
Nos chivalers e esquiers сont fait юлу н̃ homure Oye est oura(?)
pur lur beaute e leyaute que cur est anemie
le losenger puis regne le fol purpose
Sire gauwin ki poesum e sa compaigne
en sere wone en tiel amount, en payuable vie Oye est ert(?)
mes ihu est, qu ou est si must, днен enpuige arme
qe sont poure e decenus en pisone ани е
Charnel amour est folie, qe uelt amer pagemore
est holde ce qu brene uie, ne leffe duyer longement
ja nert un hete si florie que a surpert ne destent
brief odet est lechere, mes sous son duye le tourment
maim est men est qe deloite fer creuum qe child
¶ Erbe toe of erbe erbe opf bob,
¶ Erbe oper erbe to be erbe dyoh,
¶ Erbe leyde erbe morhene prob,
þo henede erbe of erbe, erbe prob,

Lystneþ Lordynges, a nelle song whulle bygynne
of þe traytors of scotlond þ take beþ þys apine. Ich underfond,
ofon hire louch felsuesse þ mise neuer ölyune
hope myn him sleđe þe hys þ be us pyne
þee wer he glad þ neuer nes afaid, of myse ne of oul,
þ wsuage bi his strotes þ bnef non to halle
he henedes o londone brugge þofe con shulde
he ondən him olten synges, ofte seiden so in syhe
liere hom were han pie bayons are like in grene latte
Whose liteth sock are psyth hered he domey sander myst þe lyeye öyng al o
to enmp alle þe germilmen þ bneþ m seue lordeis
þe walas wer to bhalte, seppe he wer an honge   To abyde
al he lihenedes þe he wales plyed
þe hened to londone brugge wer send
after symond frysel, þ wer epann arí pylel are payd ful sunde
þic edward онре ёynig þ fad pe of prece
þe lander dгет seude to ус onme tounge   Arie dyedes
en some halft to honge hueye my pont to be
þer opon to henehie þ monie myhten se
þyp wolten he be bras off þe batatle of donbar, þon ende he consppide

Early English Text Society.
ORIGINAL SERIES.

THE MIDDLE ENGLISH POEM,

Erthe upon Erthe,

PRINTED FROM TWENTY-FOUR MANUSCRIPTS,

EDITED, WITH INTRODUCTION, NOTES, AND GLOSSARY,

BY

HILDA M. R. MURRAY

Published for
THE EARLY ENGLISH TEXT SOCIETY
by the
OXFORD UNIVERSITY PRESS
LONDON   NEW YORK   TORONTO

OXFORD
UNIVERSITY PRESS

Great Clarendon Street, Oxford OX2 6DP
United Kingdom

Oxford University Press is a department of the University of Oxford.
It furthers the University's objective of excellence in research, scholarship,
and education by publishing worldwide. Oxford is a registered trade mark of
Oxford University Press in the UK and in certain other countries

© The Early English Text Society 1911

The moral rights of the authors have been asserted

Database right Oxford University Press (maker)

First Edition published in 1911
Reprinted 1964

All rights reserved. No part of this publication may be reproduced,
stored in a retrieval system, or transmitted, in any form or by any means,
without the prior permission in writing of Oxford University Press,
or as expressly permitted by law, or under terms agreed with the appropriate
reprographics rights organization. Enquiries concerning reproduction
outside the scope of the above should be sent to the Rights Department,
Oxford University Press, at the address above

You must not circulate this book in any other form
and you must impose this same condition on any acquirer

Published in the United States of America by Oxford University Press
198 Madison Avenue, New York, NY 10016, United States of America

British Library Cataloguing in Publication Data
Data available

Library of Congress Cataloging in Publication Data
Data available

Original Series, 141
ISBN 978-0-19-722141-9

To my Father

QUEM

QUAMVIS LONGISSIMO INTERVALLO

SEQUI TAMEN CONOR.

CONTENTS

	PAGE
INTRODUCTION:	
The two Versions of the Poem 'Erthe upon Erthe'	ix
Descriptive List of MSS. of the Poem	x
The **A** Version	xiv
The **B** Version	xvi
The Cambridge Text	xxv
Origin and Growth of the Poem	xxix
Later Versions of the Poem	xxxv
Literary Interest	xxxviii
Editor's Note	xli

THE **A** VERSION:

1. MS. Harleian 2253 1
2. MS. Harleian 913 1

THE **B** VERSION:

1. William Billyng's MS. 5
2. MS. Thornton 6
3. MS. Selden supra 53 7
4. MS. Egerton 1995 8
5. MS. Harleian 1671 9
6. MS. Brighton 10
7. The Stratford-on-Avon Inscription . . . 11
8. MS. Rawlinson C. 307 12
9. MS. Harleian 4486 13
10. MS. Lambeth 853 14
11. MS. Laud Miscellaneous 23 16
12. MS. Cotton Titus A. xxvi 19
13. MS. Rawlinson Poetical 32 20

CONTENTS

	PAGE
14. MS. Porkington 10	24
15. MS. Balliol 354	27
16. MS. Harleian 984	29
17. The Maitland MS.	30
18. John Reidpeth's MS.	31
THE CAMBRIDGE TEXT	32
NOTES AND ANALOGUES	35
APPENDIX:	
I. 'Erthe' Poem in Latin, French, and English (Record Office Roll, Ex^r. K. R. Proceedings, Bdle. 1, and MS. British Museum Additional 25478)	41
II. (**B** Version) additions:	
19. MS. Trinity College Cambridge R. 3. 21	47
20. MS. Trinity College Cambridge B. 15. 39	48
GLOSSARY	50

INTRODUCTION

THE TWO VERSIONS OF THE POEM 'ERTHE UPON ERTHE'.

THE Middle English poem of *Erthe upon Erthe* is one which occurs fairly frequently in fifteenth-century MSS. and even later. It was a favourite theme for Commonplace Books, and was frequently inserted on the spare leaves at the beginning or end of a manuscript. From the many texts of the poem which have survived, and from the fact that portions of it continued to be inscribed on walls and tombstones up to the beginning of the nineteenth century, a wide popularity may be deduced. The extant versions, moreover, point to a knowledge of the poem throughout the greater part of England, as well as in the south of Scotland. The grimness of the motive, based on the words *Memento homo quod cinis es et in cinerem reverteris*, allies the text both with the earlier group of poems relating to *The Soul and the Body*, and with the more or less contemporary *Dance of Death*, but whereas the two latter groups can claim a popularity which extended over western Europe, *Erthe upon Erthe* exists only in Middle English texts, and in one parallel Latin version.[1] It is, indeed, difficult to see how the play upon the word *earth* on which the poem depends could have been reproduced with equal success in any language outside English, and the Latin version is distinctly inferior in this respect. There would seem, therefore, to be good reason for the assumption that *Erthe upon Erthe* is of English origin, belonging to the same class of literature as the English versions of the *Soul and Body* poems.

The earliest texts of the poem known to be extant are found in MSS. Harleian 2253 and 913, both dated about the beginning of the fourteenth century. The two texts vary greatly in length—

[1] A second Latin version of an *Erthe* poem, together with the same poem in Anglo-French, and in Middle English, occurs on the back of a Roll in the Public Record Office, dating from the time of Edward II (Ex^r. K. R. Proceedings, Bdle. 1; old No. $\frac{645}{21}$), and in a 19th cent. transcript of this in MS. Brit. Mus. Addit. 25478; it is given in the Appendix. Both the Latin and the French appear to be translations or paraphrases of the English, with an additional verse or two.

MS. Harl. 2253 consists of four lines as against seven six-lined stanzas in MS. Harl. 913—and the latter text has the parallel Latin rendering mentioned above, but they coincide so far as they go, and appear to represent a thirteenth or fourteenth-century type of the poem, which may be called the **A** version.[1]

Another poem of the same kind, which differs considerably from the **A** version, but is, in all probability, closely connected with it in origin, is common in fifteenth-century MSS. I have traced eighteen texts of this version, dating from the fifteenth to the seventeenth century, all of which represent or are based upon the same common type, though individual transcribers appear to have expanded the theme according to their own taste. Such additions may easily be distinguished, since they seldom succeed in maintaining either the grim simplicity, or the fundamental play upon the word *earth*, which characterize the genuine portions of the poem. This common fifteenth-century type may be called the **B** version.

Lastly, a single fifteenth-century MS. (Cambridge University Library, Ii, 4. 9) has preserved a text of the poem in which some attempt seems to have been made to combine the **A** with the **B** version. This text may be called the **C** version, or Cambridge text.

In the following pages an attempt has been made to justify the premises in part laid down already, and to show that the **A** and **B** versions may be traced back to a common source, and that this source was not only confined to England, but was itself English.

MSS. OF THE POEM 'ERTHE UPON ERTHE'.

The following is a list of the manuscripts in which the poem occurs:—

MSS. of the **A** Version:

1. MS. Harl. 2253, fol. 57, v°, dated c. 1307. Four lines inserted between a French poem on the Death of Simon de Montfort, and an English poem on the Execution of Simon Fraser. Printed by J. Ritson, *Ancient Songs and Ballads from the Reign of K. Henry II to the Revolution*, p. 13 (1790), by E. Flügel, *Anglia*, xxvi. 216 (1903), and by

---

[1] The English text in the Appendix consists of nine four-lined stanzas, and is distinct from either of the two current versions of the poem. It appears to have been suggested by the opening lines of **A**, and may be regarded as a single sub-type of **A**, not affecting the main line of argument of the Introduction. (See Appendix, p. 46.)

W. Heuser, *Die Kildare-Gedichte* (*Bonner Beiträge zur Anglistik*, xiv. 179) (1904). (See the facsimile opposite the title-page.)
2. MS. Harl. 913, fol. 62, r⁰ (c. 1308–1330). Seven six-lined English stanzas alternating with seven of the same purport in Latin. Printed by T. Wright, *Reliquiae Antiquae*, ii. 216 (1841), by F. J. Furnivall, *Early Eng. Poems and Lives of Saints*, p. 150 (printed for the Philological Society, Berlin, 1862), and by W. Heuser, *ibid.*, p. 180.

MSS. of the **B** Version:

1. William Billyng's MS. (dated 1400–1430). Five four-lined stanzas, preceded by the figure of a naked body, rudely drawn, having a mattock in its right hand, and a spade at its feet. At the end of the poem is a prone figure of a skeleton accompanied by two draped figures.[1] Printed by W. Bateman, *Billyng's Five Wounds of Christ*, no. 3 (Manchester, 1814),[2] 'from a finely written and illuminated parchment roll, about two and three-quarter yards in length: it is without date, but by comparing it with other poetry, it appears to have been written early in the fifteenth century; the illuminations and ornaments with which it is decorated correspond to those of missals written about the reign of Henry V; the style may therefore fix its date between the years 1400 and 1430. The author[3] gives his name and mark at the bottom of the roll.' Reprinted from Bateman's text by J. Montgomery, *The Christian Poet*, edit. 1 and 2, p. 45 (1827), edit. 3, p. 58 (1828).
2. MS. Thornton (Lincoln Cath. Libr.), fol. 279 (c. 1440). Five stanzas[4] without mark of strophic division. Printed by G. G. Perry, *Religious Poems in Prose and Verse*, p. 95 (E. E. T. S., No. xxvi, 1867, reprinted 1889, p. 96), and by C. Horstmann, *Yorkshire Writers* (*Richard Rolle of Hampole*), i. 373 (1895).
3. MS. Selden supra 53, fol. 159, v⁰ (c. 1450). Six stanzas (strophic division indicated in the first two), written in a different hand on the back of a spare leaf at the end of the

---

[1] This is repeated on each page of Bateman's text, and is, perhaps, his own design.   [2] See Bateman's Preface.
[3] Probably not the author but the copier of the MS.: see Notes.
[4] All the stanzas of the **B** version are four-lined except MS. Porkington.

MS.; stanza 5 of the usual **B** version omitted. Quoted by H. G. Fiedler, *Modern Language Review* (April 1908), III. iii. 221. Not printed before.

4. MS. Egerton 1995, fol. 55, r⁰ (William Gregory's Commonplace Book, dated c. 1430–1450, cf. J. Gairdner, *Collections of a London Citizen*. Camden. Soc. 1876 n. s. xvii). Seven stanzas without strophic division. Not printed before.
5. MS. Harl. 1671, fol. 1*, r⁰ (fifteenth century). Seven stanzas written in the left-hand column on the fly-leaf at the beginning of the MS., which consists of a 'large Theological Treatise, imperfect at both ends, which seemeth to have been entituled "The Weye to Paradys"'.[1] The upper portion of the leaf contains a poem in praise of St. Herasmius. Not printed before.
6. MS. Brighton, fol. 90, v⁰ (fifteenth century). Seven stanzas. Printed by Fiedler, *M. L. R.* III. iii. 219, from the last leaf of a MS. formerly seen by him in possession of an antiquary at Brighton, and containing a Latin treatise on the seven Sacraments.
7. Stratford-on-Avon Inscription (after 1450). Seven stanzas, formerly on the west wall of the nave in the Chapel of the Trinity at Stratford-on-Avon, cf. R. B. Wheler, *Hist. and Antiq. of Stratford-on-Avon*, p. 98: 'against the west wall of the nave, upon the south side of the arch was painted the martyrdom of Thomas à Becket, whilst kneeling at the altar of St. Benedict in Canterbury Cathedral; below this was represented the figure of an angel (probably St. Michael) supporting a long scroll, upon which were written the following rude verses: Erth oute of erthe,' &c. 'Beneath were two men, holding another scroll over a body wrapt in a winding sheet, and covered with some emblems of mortality with these lines: Whosoo hym be thowghte,' &c. (v. Note on p. 36). These paintings were probably added in the reign of Henry VII, when the Chapel was restored by Sir Hugh Clopton (died 1496), who built New Place opposite the Chapel in 1483. They were discovered in 1804 beneath a coating of whitewash, and were copied and engraved, but have since been more than once re-coated with whitewash, and all trace of the poem has now disappeared. Facsimiles,

---

[1] v. Wanley's Catalogue.

etched and coloured by hand, exist in Thomas Fisher's *Series of Ancient Allegorical, Historical, and Legendary Paintings in fresco, discovered on the walls of the Chapel of the Trinity, belonging to the Gild of the Holy Cross, at Stratford-on-Avon, in Warwickshire, from drawings made at the time of their discovery* (1807). Printed by R. B. Wheler, *ibid.* (1806), by Longfellow, *Outre-Mer* (*Père-La-Chaise*, note on p. 67), 1851, and by W. P. Reeves, *Mod. Lang. Notes,* IX. iv. 203 (April 1894).

8. MS. Rawlinson C. 307, fol. 2, r⁰ (after 1458). Eight stanzas, of which three are peculiar to this MS., and are of a more distinctly Northern dialect than the remainder. The poem is the only English text in a MS. containing Latin prose and verse. Two Latin poems in the same hand as *Erthe upon Erthe* refer to the death of Gilbert Pynchbeck at York in 1458, which would fix the date c. 1460, or later. The three independent stanzas were printed by Fiedler, *ibid.* p. 221.

9. [1] MS. Harl. 4486, fol. 146, r⁰ (fifteenth century). Eight stanzas added on the last leaf but one of a copy of *Le Livre de Sydrac*, immediately after the colophon. The last two leaves and the cover of the MS. contain various scribblings in fifteenth-century hands, chiefly of Latin aphorisms and rimes. Folio 147, v⁰, contains the signature of Tho. Baker, who may possibly have transcribed the English poem. Not printed before.

10. MS. Lambeth 853, fol. 35 (c. 1430–1450). Twelve stanzas. Printed by F. J. Furnivall, *Hymns to the Virgin and Christ*, p. 88 (E. E. T. S. 1867, No. xxiv, reprinted 1895).

11. MS. Laud Misc. 23, fol. 111, v⁰ (before 1450). Twelve stanzas, varying very slightly from MS. Lambeth. Not printed before.

12. MS. Cotton Titus A xxvi, fol. 153, r⁰ (fifteenth century). Six four-lined stanzas, apparently the beginning of a transcript of MS. Lambeth. Not printed before.

13. MS. Rawlinson Poetic. 32, v⁰ (after 1450). Thirty-two stanzas, each of four short lines, corresponding to half the normal stanza; stanzas 17 to 30 are peculiar to this MS. The greater part printed by Fiedler, *ibid.* p. 222.

14. MS. Porkington 10, fol. 79, v⁰ (fifteenth century). Twelve six-lined stanzas, of which stanzas 7 to 11 are peculiar to

---

[1] My attention was called to this MS. by the kindness of Prof. Priebsch.

this MS. Printed by Halliwell, *Early Eng. Misc. in Prose and Verse, selected from an inedited MS. of the* 15*th cent.*, p. 39 (Warton Club, 1855), and by Fiedler, *ibid.* p. 225.

15. MS. Balliol 354, fol. 207, v⁰ (Richard Hill's Commonplace Book, dated before 1504). Sixteen stanzas, of which stanzas 6 to 14 introduce an independent digression on the Nine Worthies. Printed by Flügel, *Anglia*, xxvi. 94 (1903), and by Roman Dyboski, *Songs, Carols, and Other Misc. Poems*, p. 90 (E. E. T. S. 1907, extra ser. ci).

16. MS. Harl. 984, fol. 72, r⁰ (sixteenth century). The preceding leaf of the MS. has been torn out, leaving only two lines of what may be assumed to be verse 6, and the whole of verse 7, which occur with other fragments on the last leaf but one.

17. The Maitland MS. Pepysian Library, Magd. Coll. Cambr., MS. 2553, p. 338 (c. 1555–1585). Seven stanzas in the Lowland Scots dialect, with the ascription 'quod Marsar'. Thomas Pinkerton published portions of the MS. in his *Ancient Scottish Poems never before in print . . . from the MS. Collections of Sir Richard Maitland* (London, 1786), but omitted *Eird upon Eird.* Not printed before.

18. The Reidpeth MS. Cambridge Univ. Libr. Ll. 5. 10, fol. 43, v⁰, copied 1622–1623 'a me Joanne Reidpeth'. Seven stanzas, probably transcribed from the Maitland MS., but concluding 'quod Dumbar'. Not printed before.

MS. of the C Version:

The Cambridge Text. Cambr. Univ. Libr. Ii. 4. 9, fol. 67, r⁰ (fifteenth century). Eighty-two lines comprising twenty-two or twenty-three stanzas. The text is followed by a coloured picture of a young knight, standing on a hill with a skeleton below. A scroll proceeding from the knight has the words: *Festina tempus et memento finis*, while one proceeding from the skeleton runs: *In omni opere memorare nouissima et in eternum non peccabis.* Printed by Heuser, *Kildare-Gedichte*, p. 213.

The A Version.

The **A** version exists in two forms, one a short popular stanza of four lines (MS. Harl. 2253), apparently of the nature of a riddle, the other a longer poem of seven English and seven Latin stanzas (MS. Harl. 913), each English verse being followed by its

Latin equivalent. The metrical form of the Latin verses is one often used in Latin poems of the twelfth and thirteenth centuries, a six-lined stanza, rimed *aaaabb*, with the rhythm of the well-known

méum ést propósitúm | *in tabérna móri.*

The English verses are also in the form of a six-lined stanza *aaaabb*, but the first four lines have the same loose four-stress rhythm as the lines in MS. Harl. 2253, and the concluding couplet is on the principle of the septenarius. Both the English and the Latin lines rime at the caesura as well as at the end of the line, but this is less uniformly the rule in the English verses. There is close verbal connexion between the four lines in MS. Harl. 2253, and the opening lines of the longer poem, as will appear from a comparison of the two:—

MS. Harl. 2253.

  Erþe toc of erþe   erþe wyþ woh
  erþe oþer erþe   to þe erþe droh
  erþe leyde erþe   in erþene þroh
  þo heuede erþe of erþe   erþe ynoh

MS. Harl. 913.

  whan erþ haþ erþ . iwonne wiþ wow
  þan erþ mai of erþ . nim hir inow
  erþ vp erþ . falliþ fol frow
  erþ toward erþ . delful him drow.
  of erþ þou were makid . and mon þou art ilich
  in on erþ awaked . þe pore and þe riche.

The connexion between these two versions might be explained in two ways. The short version of MS. Harl. 2253 may be the beginning of a transcript of the longer poem in which the scribe broke off because his memory failed him, or because he was only acquainted with a popular version of the opening lines. On the other hand, the short version may be the older, and the more learned composer of the poem in MS. Harl. 913 may have been elaborating this and other such riddling stanzas current at the time. But any attempt to decide between these two possibilities must necessarily depend upon the conclusion formed as to the relation of the Latin stanzas in MS. Harl. 913 to their English equivalents, and this question will be more conveniently discussed in connexion with the general origin of the *Erthe upon Erthe* poems. As regards the date of the two MSS., MS. Harl. 2253 is generally ascribed to the beginning of the fourteenth century, and the Kildare MS. (MS. Harl. 913) is dated c. 1308 by Crofton Croker, c. 1308 to 1330 by Heuser, while Paul Meyer is of opinion that it may belong to an earlier period still. The dialect of both poems is South Midland, probably of the western part of the district. MS. Harl. 2253, which is commonly associated with Leominster, has *heuede* (4). MS. Harl. 913 has *lutil, schrud, muntid, heo, mon, lond,* and S. Midl. forms of verbs. We have therefore two types of the **A** version, standing in close verbal relation to each other, of much the same date and dialect, and representing in all probability the kind of *Erthe* poem current at the end of the thirteenth century in the South-west Midland district.

THE B VERSION.

As will appear from the foregoing account of the MSS., the eighteen texts of the **B** version vary considerably in length, many of them introducing stanzas which do not recur elsewhere. A comparison of the number and arrangement of the stanzas in each text is given on the next page, the stanzas being numbered according to the order of their arrangement in the text to which they belong, and the corresponding stanzas in the various texts grouped under columns. MSS. Thornton, Selden, and Egerton have no mark of strophic division, but fall naturally into mono-rimed stanzas of four lines. All the remaining texts are arranged in four-lined stanzas with mono-rime,[1] with the exception of MS. Porkington, which represents an evident expansion of the original metrical scheme, an additional long line being attached to each stanza by means of a short bob-line, giving a six-lined stanza, *aaaabb*. In MS. Rawl. Poet. each long line is written as two short lines, so that the usual four-lined stanza appears in this text as two stanzas, each consisting of four half-lines. This arrangement is facilitated by the regular internal rime on the word *erthe*. The order of the fifteenth-century MSS. of the **B** version observed in the table corresponds to that in the foregoing list of MSS., and in the printed text, and is not always strictly chronological, it being more convenient for purposes of comparison to group the texts according to their length. It will be seen that the three late texts (MSS. Harl. 984, Maitland, and Reidpeth) revert to the normal seven-stanza type, and that this appears to have been the form of the poem known to the compiler of the Cambridge text, a comparison of which is added.

---

[1] MS. Laud Misc. is not written throughout in metrical lines, but the divisions of the stanzas, and, in most cases, of the lines, are clearly indicated.

INTRODUCTION. xvii

Text.	Common Stanzas.										Independent Stanzas.
1. Wm. Billyng's Text	1	2	3	4	5						
2. MS. Thornton	1	2	3	4	5						
3. MS. Selden, supra 53	1	2	3	5		4	6				
4. MS. Egerton 1995	1	2	3	4	5	6	7				
5. MS. Harl. 1671	1	2	3	4	5	6	7				
6. MS. Brighton	1	2	3	4	5	6	7				
7. Stratford Inscription	1	2	3	4	5	6	7				
8. MS. Rawl. C. 307	1	2.	3	4	5		7	8			stanzas 6. 7. 8. (3)
9. MS. Harl. 4486	1	2	3	4	5	6	7	8			
10. MS. Lambeth 853	1	2	3	4	8	9	11	12	5	6	7	10
11. MS. Laud Misc. 23	1	2	3	4	8	9	11	12	5	6	7	10
12. MS. Cotton Titus A. xxvi	1. 2.	3. 4.	6. 5.	7. 8.					5	6		
13. MS. Rawl. Poet.					11. 12.			31. 32.	15. 16.		9. 10.	13. 14	17 to 30. (14)
14. MS. Porkington 10	1	2	3	4	5	6	12					7 to 11 (5)
15. MS. Balliol 354	1	2	3	4	5	15	16					6 to 14 (9)
16. MS. Harl. 984 [1]	(1)	(2)	(3)	(4)	(5)	6	7					
17. MS. Maitland	1	2	3	4	5	6	7					(6. 7. 13-18 resemble A Version. 4-5. 12. 14 to 17. 19 to 22 independent (11)
18. MS. Reidpeth	1	2	3	4	5	6	7					
The Cambridge Text	1	3. 8.	2	10	9	11						

[1] The first leaf of this text has been torn out and the verses in brackets are only conjectural.

It will be seen from the table that eleven of these texts have seven stanzas in common, and that fifteen of them have five in common. Of the three remaining texts, MS. Harl. 984 has a missing leaf, but would clearly appear to belong to the seven-stanza type, raising the above numbers to twelve texts of seven stanzas, and sixteen of five. MS. Selden again obviously represents the usual seven-stanza type with the accidental omission of verse 5. MS. Titus has four of the customary five verses, breaks off to follow the arrangement of the Lambeth MS., and comes to an end after copying two of the additional verses in the Lambeth text before reaching the usual fifth verse. Assuming that it represents a transcription of the Lambeth text, MS. Titus might be classed with the five-stanza type, or possibly, like MS. Lambeth, with the seven-stanza type. It may therefore be assumed that all eighteen of the B texts have five stanzas in common, or are based upon such a common type, and that thirteen, or possibly fourteen of them, represent a common type with seven stanzas, six of which are further found in the Cambridge text. These common stanzas vary very little in the different MSS. as regards either the actual text or the order of lines and stanzas, and it seems probable that the normal B version consisted of seven stanzas, ending with a personal exhortation which has been omitted, or possibly not yet added, in five of the texts. In four MSS.—Lambeth, Laud, Rawl. P., and Harl. 4486—an interesting final stanza, containing a prayer, has been added. Three of these texts, MSS. Lamb., Laud, and Rawl. P., correspond in three other additional stanzas, which seems to point to some closer relationship between them, and two, or more strictly one and a half, of these additional stanzas are also found in MS. Titus, which appears to be a transcript of the Lambeth text. The scribe of MS. Titus followed the Lambeth text until he reached the middle of verse 6, when he apparently wearied of the task, and broke off with a new couplet of his own, entirely foreign in idea and metre to the *Erthe upon Erthe* poems :—

> Lewe thy syne & lyffe in right,
> And þan shalt thou lyffe in heuyn as a knyght.

The text, as a whole, is badly written with many erasures, and points to a careless hand.

The additional stanzas cited in the table as independent contain

mere variations on the main theme, and it is highly probable that
the more expanded texts are the later, and represent individual
additions to a popular poem, since they generally fail to maintain
the internal rime on the word *erthe* which is an evident character-
istic of the genuine verses. In the case of the five MSS. in
question, MS. Harl. 4486 might be taken to represent the original
type, and MSS. Lamb., Laud [1], and Titus an expansion of this, while
the author of Rawl. P. was obviously acquainted with the Lambeth
text, or its original, and added to it certain stanzas of his own,
leaving out three of the verses in Lambeth to make room for these.
Whether the eighth stanza which MSS. Harl. 4486, Lamb., Laud,
and Rawl. P. have in common belongs to the original type of the B
version, or was itself a later addition, can scarcely be determined,
but as it seems to be confined to these four texts, the latter view is
perhaps the more probable. It must, however, have been added
early, as it occurs already in MSS. Lamb. and Laud before 1450, and
preserves the principle of the internal rime on *erthe*. The relative
dates of MSS. Lambeth and Rawl. P. as fixed by Furnivall and
Madden (MS. Lamb. 1430–1450, R. P. after 1450) would bear out
this theory of the relationship between these two texts, and it may
further be noted that both have the same prefatory *De terra plas-
masti me*, otherwise found only in MS. Harl. 1671, and that both
exhibit the same tendency to employ a direct personal mode of
address, and to lengthen out the original text by superfluous words.

Cf. for example, MS. Harl. 4486, verse 5 (so MS. Laud,
verse 8)—

> Why erthe loueth erthe wonder me thynke,
> Or why that erthe for erthe swete wylle or swynke, &c.

with MS. Lamb. verse 8—

> Whi þat erþe *to myche* loueþ erþe, wondir me þink,
> Or whi þat erþe for *superflue* erþe *to sore* sweete wole or swynk

and MS. Rawl. P. verse 11—

> Or whi that erthe for the erthe
> *Unresonably* swete wol or swynke.

---

[1] MS. Laud represents, in the main, the same version as MS. Lamb., but
the variant readings preclude the idea of its being a copy of Lamb., unless the
scribe deliberately tried to modify his original on the lines of Harl. 4486 and
Rawl. P. The changes in the text (ll. 26, 27, 47: see Notes) show that it cannot
be the original of Lamb. It appears to be a transcript from the same original
made about the same date, or a little earlier than the Lambeth text.

The exact date of the text in MS. Titus is indeterminate, but, as stated above, it is evidently based on MS. Lambeth or its original, and might be ascribed to c. 1450 or later. The text in MS. Harl. 4486 has been added by some later owner of the MS. on the last leaves of a fifteenth-century transcript of *Le Livre de Sydrac*. The handwriting of *Erthe upon Erthe* is also fifteenth century, but the exact date again cannot be determined. The text, however, is far simpler and nearer to the original than that of the other four MSS., and evidently represents an earlier type than these, though the actual transcript may be later.

With the exception of these five MSS., it is not easy to group the eighteen texts of the B version on any system based upon the additional stanzas, since these fail to bear out any theory as to closer relationship between individual MSS., though the connexion of ideas is often close owing to the similarity of the theme. Thus the nine additional stanzas in MS. Balliol contain a digression upon the nine worthies with an interesting reference in verse 12 to the Dance of Powlis, i.e. the Dance of Death formerly depicted outside St. Paul's Cathedral (v. Notes, p. 36). It is in the Cambridge text alone that the additional stanzas supply an interesting connexion with the A version, which places this text, unfortunately corrupt and difficult to decipher, in an important position as a link between A and B.

With regard to possible relationships dependent upon variations in the order or arrangement of the lines in the seven common stanzas, it may be pointed out that the first verse in MS. Egerton consists of three lines only, the usual second line being omitted, and that both MS. Harl. 1671 and MS. Porkington omit the same line, though each of these supplies a new and independent fourth line to fill the gap:—

(*MS. Egerton* 1995)

    Erthe owte of þe erthe ys wounderly wrought,
    Erthe vppon erthe hathe sette hys thought
    How erthe a-pon erthe may be hy brought.

(*MS. Harl.* 1671)

    Erthe apon erthe ys waxyne and wrought,
    And erthe apon erthe hathe ysette all hys thought
    How that erth apon erth hye myght be brought,
    But how that erth scal to the erth thyngketh he noht.

(*MS. Porkington* 10)
  Erthe vppon eithe is woundyrely wrouȝte ;
  Erthe vppon erthe has set al his þouȝte
  How erthe vppon erth to erthe schall be brouȝte ;
  There is none vppon erth has hit in þouȝte.
      Take hede!
  Whoso þinkyse on his ende, ful welle schal he spede.

It is obvious that these new lines are an afterthought, especially in the case of MS. Porkington, where the rime-word *þouȝte* has to be repeated. Possibly these three texts depend upon a common original in which the usual second line *Erth hath gotyn vppon erth a dygnyte of noght* was lacking, or MS. Egerton may have been the original of the other two. But MS. Harl. 1671 varies from the other two in the first line also, using a version which is otherwise confined to the Cambridge text—

  Erthe apon erthe ys *waxyne and* wrought—

and both it and MS. Porkington begin *erthe upon erthe* like the later texts, as opposed to the more usual *erthe owte of erthe*, so that there is no clear evidence of a closer relationship between these three texts.

In verse 4, again, an inversion of the customary order of the second or third lines is common to MSS. Rawl. C., Porkington, Maitland, Reidpeth, and the Stratford-on-Avon inscription, but the verse easily lends itself to transposition of the kind, and in MS. Rawl. C. the usual first line is also put third, so that the order of lines as compared with the normal arrangement becomes 2. 3. 1. 4. Beyond the self-evident fact that the Maitland and Reidpeth MSS. must be grouped together, no relationship of the MSS. can be deduced from this transposition, though it may point to a second popular version with inversion of lines 2 and 3.

One of the most important differences of reading in the common stanzas occurs in the first line of the poem, where twelve of the eighteen MSS. read *erthe out of erthe*, while the remaining six, as well as the Cambridge text, have *erthe upon erthe.* Three of these six are definitely later transcripts: MS. Porkington is obviously a later modification of the original four-lined stanza, and MSS. Maitland and Reidpeth belong to the late sixteenth and early seventeenth centuries respectively ; the beginning of MS. Harl. 984

is not preserved, and the remaining two texts, MSS. Selden and Harl. 1671, belong to c. 1450, while the Cambridge text, as will be shown later, cannot be regarded as original. Evidently *erthe owt of erthe* was the original reading, but the version *erthe upon erthe* was introduced early, and appears to have survived the other. A similar change occurs in the last line of verse 2, where MS. Harl. 1671 and the Stratford text substitute *erth upon erth* for *out of, from, of*, of the other texts, and again in the third line of verse 4 (l. 2 in the texts mentioned above as transposing these lines) where the same two MSS. read *erth upon erth* for the normal *erth unto (into, to) erthe*; also in the fourth line of verse 7, where MSS. Harl. 4486, Lamb., Laud, Maitland, and Reidpeth read *upon* for *owte of*. Now the last two lines of the first verse of the poem invariably use the phrase *erth upon erthe*, and it occurs repeatedly throughout the poem as a synonym for *man*: e. g. verse 2, line 1; 3, ll. 1, 3; 4, ll. 1, 2 (or 3); 5, l. 3; 6, ll. 1, 3; 7, l. 1. It was very natural that the common phrase, and the one best adapted to serve as a title to the poem, should tend to replace others, but it seems probable that wherever the substitution occurs it may be taken as due to a later tradition, and consequently as a proof of non-originality or comparative lateness in the text in which it is found. A similar change, and one to be explained in a similar way, is the introduction of *wonderly* for *wyckydly* in the first line of verse 7 on the analogy of the first line of the poem, which occurs in MSS. Harl. 1671 and Stratford, and also in the late MSS. Maitland and Reidpeth.

Other variations of reading are less noteworthy. In the second line of verse 1, ten MSS., ranging from the early Thornton and Lambeth to the late Maitland and Reidpeth, read *dignite*, while the others vary between *nobley* (MS. Brighton, cf. the Cambridge text), *nobul þyng* (Billyng), *worschyp* (Selden), and *an abbey*, perhaps an error for *nobley* (Harl. 4486). The remaining three MSS. omit the line. In the fourth line of verse 2, the alliterative *piteous parting* of MSS. Billyng, Egerton, Brighton, Harl. 4486, Lamb., Laud, Titus, and Rawl. P., is replaced by *hard parting* not only in the Stratford text and in the later MSS. (Porkington, Balliol, Maitland, Reidpeth), but also in MSS. Thornton and Rawl. C., while other readings are *dolful* (MS. Selden, cf. the Cambridge text) and *heuy* (MS. Harl. 1671). It is difficult here to decide between *piteous* and *hard*, but the preference should probably rest with the alliterative phrase. In the fourth line of verse 3, the alliterative *scharpe schowres* is evidently the original reading, and it occurs in all texts except Stratford, Rawl. P., and Balliol.

In the first line of verse 4, *erthe goeth upon erthe as moulde upon moulde* occurs in thirteen texts, and two others (Stratford and Balliol, cf. also the Cambridge text) keep the rime *mould* while altering the line. The other two readings found, *colde opon colde* (Rawl. C.), and *golde appone golde* (Thornton), are obviously non-original, particularly the latter, which repeats the rime-word *gold* in two successive lines.

Other variations and occasional transpositions of lines occur in individual MSS., but are unimportant.

It will thus be seen that the popular traditional version of the poem tended to become modified, and even corrupt, already in the fifteenth century, and that such modifications are usually more apparent in the later texts. It is also evident that individual transcribers felt themselves at liberty to expand the traditional version, and that many tried their hand at such variations on the original theme, but the striking absence of proof of relationship outside the seven stanzas of the normal version, as well as the frequent unimportant variations found in the common stanzas, seems to point clearly to the conclusion that the original was a popular poem of seven, or possibly only five, stanzas, widely known over England, and that the more simple and naïve of the seventeen texts extant are also more genuine, and nearer to the original.

Many of the texts are accompanied by a short prefatory or concluding verse in English or Latin. The English verse—

When lyffe is most loued, and deth is moste hated,
Then dethe draweth his drawght and makyth man fall naked

occurs as a preface in MSS. Harl. 4486 and 1671, Lambeth, Laud, Rawl. P., and Egerton, and as a conclusion in Billyng's text. The Latin *Memento homo quod cinis es et in cinerem reverteris* occurs, in full or in part, in MSS. Harl. 4486, Egerton, Rawl. C., Lambeth, and Billyng, and *De terra plasmasti me* in MSS. Harl. 1671, Lambeth, and Rawl. P. The two stanzas in rime royal on the *Proces of Dethe* which immediately precede *Erthe upon Erthe* in the Porkington MS. are transcribed as a separate poem, and if not separate, would rather belong to the preceding text, a translation of the Latin *Visio Philiberti* in rime royal, than to *Erthe upon Erthe*. The latter poem often accompanies either a *Dance of Death* or one of the numerous *Soul and Body* dialogues, no doubt because of the similarity of the theme, but it is not necessary to regard these kindred poems as forming an essential part of each other. So in the Balliol MS., *Erthe upon Erthe* is preceded by an eight-lined Latin stanza on the theme *vado mori*, which is probably part of a *Dance of Death*. Here again no basis for a grouping of the MSS. can be found.

The two late texts—MSS. Maitland and Reidpeth—represent a Lowland Scots version of the poem, and are obviously copies of the same original. Probably the Reidpeth text is a transcription of the Maitland, but it contains some obvious misreadings of it, as in verse 3, line 3, *bowris* (Maitl.), *towris* (Reidpeth) repeating the rime-word; 5, l. 20, *within* (Maitl.), *with* (Reidpeth). The Maitland MS., compiled c. 1555–1585, adds the colophon *quod Marsar*. The later Reidpeth MS., 1622–1623, concludes with the words *quod Dumbar*. Mersar, or Marsar, is mentioned in Dunbar's *Lament for the Makaris*, and is usually identified with a William Mersar of the household of James IV, mentioned 1500 to 1503. In any case, if he were a contemporary of Dunbar, he could scarcely be assigned to a sufficiently early date to account for the widespread popularity of *Erthe upon Erthe* all over England in 1450, and the fact that the two MSS. assign the poem to different authors, of whom Dunbar is manifestly impossible, and Mersar at least improbable, may be explained as an instance of that readiness of posterity to attach a known name to a work of unknown origin, of which other examples are not wanting. It is, however, of interest to find that the poem had made its way to Scotland by 1550 or thereabouts.

As regards dialect, the majority of the MSS. of the **B** version show traces of Northern dialect, most of them preserving the Nth. plural in -*is* in the rimes *touris*, *schowrys*, &c. In verse 3 also the majority of the texts have the Nth. *bigged* or *biggid*, but six (MSS. Billyng, Egerton, Rawl. P., Porkington, Balliol, and the Stratford text) use the Midl. or Sth. *bilded* or *billed*. In verse 4 the rime requires the form *wold* rather than the common Nth. *wald*, and even the Maitland MS. retains *wold* for the sake of the rime, whereas MS. Reidpeth substitutes *wald*, sacrificing the rime.

MSS. Thornton and Rawl. C. show distinct Nth. features, such as the verb-endings -*is* (pres. ind. 3 sg.), -*and* (pres. part.), -*id*, -*it*, -*in* (past part.), and MS. Rawl. C. has the Nth. *whate gates at þu gase* riming with *fase* (*foes*). But few of the MSS. represent pure dialect-forms, and an investigation of the dialect of the texts is of little assistance towards determining that of the original poem. Such evidence as exists points, on the whole, to the North Midland district, and a widespread popularity in the North, which led to the later knowledge of the poem across the Border, but the popularity was evidently not confined to the North, and Southern as well as Northern forms may be traced in both early and late transcripts.

The Cambridge Text.

The Cambridge MS., as has been already stated, combines portions of both the **A** and the **B** version with several independent stanzas. At first sight it might appear to represent a transitional stage in the development of the **B** from the **A** type, but closer examination shows that this is not the case, and that the text is merely a later compilation from the two. The writer must have had some knowledge both of the longer **A** version represented by MS. Harl. 913, and of the common seven-stanza **B** type, and seems to have tried to combine his recollections in one poem, halting between the four-lined and six-lined stanza, repeating himself here and there, and adding certain new verses of his own. There is no grouping into stanzas in the MS., but a division is easily made by the rimes, and these give mono-rimed stanzas of four lines chiefly, with one of six lines, and some fragmentary ones of two or three. In one case a stanza has been broken up and the two couplets inserted at different points (ll. 9–10, 27–28). As has been shown in the table of MSS. of the **B** version, six verses of the **B** type may be traced, while four verses show distinct correspondence with **A**, and eleven are independent of either. A comparison of the similar lines follows:—

(*MS. Cambr.* Ii. 4. 9) ll. 1–4.	(*MS. Harl.* 4486.) **B** Version.
Erthe vpon erthe is waxin & wrought,	1 Erthe owte of erthe is wonderly wrowghte,
Erthe takys on erthe a noby-lay of nought;	Erthe of the erthe hathe gete an abbey [1] of nawte,

[1] *Cf. MS. Brighton* nobley.

(Cambr.)

    Now erthe vpon erthe layes
all his þought
How erthe vpon erthe sattys
all at noght.

ll. 9–10, 27–28.

    Erthe vpon erth wolde be a kyng,
But howe erth xal to erth
thynkyth he no thyng.
When erthe says to erth: 'My
rent þou me bryng,'
Then has erth fro erthe a
dolfull partyng.

ll. 5–8.

    Erthe vpon erth has hallys &
towris;
Erthe says to erth: 'This is
alle owris.'
But quan erth vpon erth has
byggyd his bowris
Than xal erth for the erth
haue scharpe schowris.

Cf. l. 66.

    If erth haue mys don, he getyth
scharpe shours.

ll. 33–35.

    Erthe wrotys in erth as molys
don in molde,
Erthe vpon erth glydys as
golde,
As erthe leve in erthe euer
more schulde.

ll. 29–32.

    How erthe louys erth wondyr
me thynke,
How erthe for erth wyll swete
and swynke.
When erth is in erthe broght
with-in the brynke
What as herth than of erth'e
but a fowle stynke.

(B Version)

    Erthe apon erthe hath sette al
his thowghte
How erthe apon erthe may be
hye browte.

2 Erthe apon erthe be he a kynge,
Butt how erth schalle to erthe
thynkethe he nothynge.
When erthe byddeth erthe his
rent home brynge,
Then schalle erthe owte of
erthe haue a pyteous[1]
partynge.

3 Erthe apon erthe wynneth
castelles & towres.
Then seythe erthe to erthe:
'These bythe alle owres.'
When erthe apon erthe hath
byggede vp his bowres
Then schalle erthe for the erthe
suffre scharpe schowres.

4 Erthe gothe apon erthe as
molde apon molde.
So goeth erthe apon erthe alle
gleterynge in golde,
Lyke as erthe into erthe neuer
go scholde,
And ȝet schalle erthe into erthe
rather then he wolde.

5 Why erthe louethe erthe wonder me thynke,
Or why that erthe for erthe
swete wylle or swynke,
Ffor whan erthe apon erthe is
browte withyn þe brynke,
Then schalle erthe of the erthe
haue a fowle stynke.

[1] *Cf. MS. Selden* delful.

INTRODUCTION.

(Cambr.)　　　　　　　　　(B Version)

ll. 36-37.

 Erthe vpon erth mynd euer more þou make
 How erthe xal to erth when deth wyll hym take.

6 Loo erthe apon erthe con-sydere thow may
 How erthe commyth to erthe naked all way.

(*MS. Harl.* 913) **A** Version.

ll. 19-22.

 Erth vpon erthe gos in the weye,
 Prykys and prankys on a palfreye ;
 When erth has gotyn erth alle that he maye,
 He schal haue but seven fote at his last daye.

v. 5, ll. 1, 2, 5, 6.

 Erþ is a palfrei to king and to quene,
 Erþ is ar lang wei, þouw we lutil wene.
 Whan erþ haþ erþ wiþ streinþ þus geten,
 Alast he haþ is leinþ miseislich i-meten.

ll. 41-46, 23-26.

 Ffor erth gos in erth walkand in vede,
 And erthe rydys on erth on a fayr stede,
 When he was gotyn in erth erth to his mede,
 Than is erth layde in erthe wormys to fede.
 Whylke are the wormys the flesch brede ?
 God wote the wormys for to ryght rede.
 Than xal not be lykyng vnto hym
 Bu[t] an olde sely cloth to wynde erthe in,
 When erthe is in erth for wormys wyn,
 The rof of his hows xal ly on his chyn.

v. 2.

 Erþ geþ on erþ wrikkend in weden,
 Erþ toward erþ wormes to feden ;
 Erþ berriþ to erþ al is lif deden ;
 When erþ is in erþe, heo muntid þi meden.
 When erþ is in erþe, þe rof is on þe chynne ;
 Þan schullen an hundred wormes wroten on þe skin.

ll. 63-64.

 Erthe bygyth hallys & erth bygith towres,
 When erth is layd in erth, blayke is his bours ;

v. 6, ll. 5-6.

 Erþ bilt castles, and erþe bilt toures ;
 Whan erþ is on erþe, blak beþ þe boures.

l. 38.

 Be ware, erth, for erthe, for sake of thi sowle.

v. 6, l. 3.

 Erþ uppon erþ be þi soule hold.

The additional verses in MS. Cambr. bear some slight resemblance to other additional lines found in MSS. of the **B** type, and this is interesting as showing that the writer worked on the same lines in expanding his text, and was perhaps acquainted with some of the longer **B** texts. On the other hand characteristic differences in the treatment of the theme would seem to support the view that these verses are really individual additions and not derived from any of the other texts. The lines in question are given below:—

MS. Cambr. ll. 71–82.
    God walkyd in erth as longe
        as he wolde,
    He had not in this erth but
        hong*er* & colde,
    And in this erth also his body
        was solde,
    Here in this erth, whan þat
        he was xxx^{ti} ʒer*e* olde.

    God lytyd in erth, blyssed be
        that stou*n*de!
    He sauyd hijs herth w*ith* many
        a scharpe wou*n*de,
    Ffor to sawe erth owght of
        hell grou*n*de,
    He deyd in erth vpon þe rode
        w*ith* many a blody vou*n*de.

    And God ros ovght of the est
        this erth for to spede,
    And went into hell as was
        gret nede,
    And toke erth from sorowe þ*is*
        erth for to spede,
    The ryght wey to heuen blys
        I*esus* Cryst vs lede!

MS. Rawl. C. v. 8.
    Now he þat erthe opon erthe
        ordande to go
    Graunt þat erthe vpon erthe
        may govern hym so,
    Þat when erthe vnto erthe
        shalle be taken to,
    Þat þe saule of þis erthe suffre
        no wo.

MS. Rawl. P. vv. 31, 32.
    Lord God that erthe tokist in
        erthe,
    And suffredist paynes ful
        stille,
    Late neuer erthe for the erthe
        In dedly synne ne spille.

    But that erthe in this erthe
    Be doynge euer thi wille,
    So that erthe for the erthe
    Stye up to thi holi hille.
    (Cf. Harl. 4486, v. 8;
    Lamb. v. 12; Laud v.
    12).

It is therefore evident that the Cambridge text shows knowledge of both the **A** and the **B** versions, but the text in its existing form must represent either a corrupt copy of the original with frequent dislocation of lines, or, what is perhaps more likely from the instances of repetition of the same words or ideas which occur, a clumsy compilation from the two made by some one who perhaps had **B** before him and remembered portions of **A** imper-

INTRODUCTION. xxix

fectly. Such repetitions occur in verses 2 and 18, the latter repeating three of the rime-words of the former verse, as well as the phrase *scharpe schowris*; and again in verses 4 and 19, and in verses 6, 7, and 13. In any case the text must be regarded as later than the **A** and **B** versions, and not as forming a link between them. The dialect is Northern, but not uniformly so.

Origin and Growth of the Poem.

The question as to the source of the poem *Erthe upon Erthe*, and the relationship of the **A** and **B** versions to the original, and to each other, is a difficult one. The existence of a parallel Latin version in one of the oldest MSS. is clearly an important point to be taken into consideration in any attempt at an investigation of the origin of the poem, and it will be well before proceeding further to form some conclusion as to the relation in which the English and Latin stanzas in MS. Harl. 913 stand to each other. The correspondence of the two versions is not strictly verbal, but it is evident that either the English or the Latin stanzas represent a rather free rendering of the verses which accompany them. In favour of a Latin origin it may be pointed out that the metrical form of the Latin stanzas is one frequently employed in Latin poems of the time, that the subject is a favourite monastic theme, and that the manner of the poem is in keeping with contemporary Anglo-Latin compositions, such as the well-known *Cur mundus militat sub vana gloria*. The natural tendency would be to attribute a poem of the kind to Latin origin, especially if, as in this case, a Latin version were forthcoming.

On the other hand, it may be pointed out that the Latin text is not known to exist in any other MS., and appears indeed to have no separate existence from the English stanzas which accompany it, whereas English texts of the poem without trace of a Latin rendering or original are very common.[1] The text was one frequently used in epitaphs, but no Latin epitaph of the kind is known to have existed, although Latin was commonly used in epitaphs at the time when the poem was most widely popular.

Further, word-plays of the kind found here upon the word *erthe* are certainly not common in Latin verse of the time, and the Latin

---

[1] The Latin and Anglo-French texts in the Appendix are evidently renderings of the English poem which accompanies them.

text does not render the play as effectively as the English does, employing alternately the three terms *terra, vesta, humus*, in place of the English *erthe*, and failing to maintain these consistently. The play on the word *earth*, which is the most essential feature of the poem, could not have been given with the same effect as in English either in Latin or in any mediaeval language.[1]

Thirdly, in support of an English origin it may be urged that close verbal connexion can be traced between the English text of both versions, but more especially of the earlier (**A**), and other poems dating from the twelfth to the fifteenth century, particularly the various Dialogues of *The Soul and the Body* :—

MS. Harl. 913, l. 17 (**A**).
    When erþ is in erþe, þe rof is on þe chynne.

MS. Cambr. Univ. Libr. Ii. 4. 9, l. 25 (**C**)
    When erthe is in erth for wormys wyn,
    Þe rof of his hows xal ly on his chyn.

Cf. *Dialogues of Soul and Body.*
    (*Worcester fragment*) 12th cent.
    'nu þu havest neowe hus inne beþrungen, lowe beoþ helewes.
    Þin rof liþ on þine breoste, ful ... colde is þe ibedded.
    (*Bodl. Fragm.*) 12th cent.
    Þe rof biðˋ ibyld þire broste ful neh.
    (*MS. Auchinleck*) 13th cent.
    Wiþ wormes is now ytaken þin in,
    Þi bour is bilt wel cold in clay,
    Þe rof *shal take to*[2] þi chin.
    (*MS. Harl.* 2253) 14th cent.
    When þe flor is at þy rug,
    Þe rof ys at þy neose.
    Cf. *Death* 152 (13th cent.) in Morris, *O. E. Misc.*, p. 168 (*Jesus MS.*).
    Þi bur is sone ibuld
      Þat þu schalt wunyen inne,
    Þe rof *& þe virste*[3]
      Schal ligge on þine chynne.
    Nu þe schulen wurmes
      Wunyen wiþinne.

---

[1] This is clearly seen in the Latin and French versions in the Appendix where the Latin text uses *terra in terra*, and the French *terre en terre*.
[2] *Vernon MS.* to resten on, *Digby*, shal rest right at.
[3] *Cotton MS.* þe rof þe firste.

INTRODUCTION.

MS. Harl. 913, l. 66 (**A**).
   Erþ bilt castles, & erþe bilt toures;
   Whan erþ is on erþe, blak beþ þe boures.

MS. Harl. 4486 (**B**); *so other* **B** *texts.*
   Erthe apon erthe wynnethe castelles & towres.
   Then seythe erthe to erthe:
     'These bythe alle owres'.
   When erthe apon erthe hath byggede vp his bowres,
   Then schalle erthe for the erthe suffre scharpe schowres.

MS. Cambr. 63 (**C**).
   Erthe bygyth hallys & erth bygith towres,
   When erþ is layd in erth, blayke is his bours;

ibid. 5–8
   Erthe vpon erthe has hallys & towris &c.

MS. Harl. 913. 42 (**A**).
   Be þou þre niȝt in a þrouȝ, þi frendschip is ilor.[1]

Cf. *Soul & Body Dialogues* (*MSS.* Auchinleck, Digby, Vernon, Laud).
   Whare be þine castels & þine tours,
   Þine chaumbres & þine heiȝe halle,
   . . . . . .
   Wrecche, ful derk it is þi bour
   To morn þou schalt þerin falle.
(*ibid.*)
   Halles heiȝe & bours briȝt
   Y hadde y bilt & mirþes mo.

(*MS. Harl.* 2253).
   thi castles & thy toures.

Cf. *Death* 29.
   Ah seoþþen mony mon
   By-yet bures & halle,
   Forþi þe wrecche soule
   Schal into pyne falle.

Cf. *Visio Philiberti* (*MS.* Porkington).
   When þou art dede þi frenschype is aslepe.

Cf. *Soul & Body* (*MS.* Auchinleck).
   that alle þine frend beon fro þe fledde.

Cf. *Death* 97.
   Hwer beoð alle þine freond
   Þet fayre þe bi-hehte
   And fayre þe igretten
   Bi weyes and bi strete.
   Nu heo walleþ wrecche
   Alle þe forlete
   Nolde heo non herestonkes[2]
   Nu þe imete.

---
[1] Cf. *Frendles ys þe dede* (*Proverbs of Hendyng*, l. 288).
[2] = heres þonkes, *of their own free will.*

MS. Cambr. 1. 21 (C).
   When erth has gotyn erthe
     alle that he maye
   He schal haue but seven fote
     at his laste daye.

Cf. *Soul & Body* (*MSS. Auchinl., Digby*).
   Now schaltow haue at al þi
     siþe
   Bot seuen fet, vnneþe þat.

The play upon the word *earth* recurs in other English poems. Cf. *A Song on the Times* (MS. Harl. 913), early fourteenth century—

    [1] Whan erthe hath erthe i-gette
      And of erthe so hath i-nouȝ,
     When he is therin i-stekke,
      Wo is him that was in wouȝ.

where the idea and the two rime-words are the same as in *MS. Harl.* 2253—

     Erþe toc of erþe erþe wyþ woh,
     Erþe oþer erþe to þe erþe droh,
     Erþe leyde erþe in erþene þroh,
     þo heuede erþe of erþe erþe ynoh.

It will be remembered that these two MSS. (Harl. 913 and 2253) are the two which preserve texts of the **A** version, and the opening lines of the *Song on the Times* would appear to give further proof of a connexion between the two **A** texts.

Further, in *MS. Lansdowne* 762 (v. *Reliquiae Antiquae* I. 260), under the heading *Terram terra tegat*, occur these lines:—

    First to the erthe I bequethe his parte,
    My wretched careyn is but fowle claye,
    Like than to like, erthe in erthe to laye;
    Sith it is, according by it I wolle abide,
    As for the first parte of my wille, that erthe erthe hide.

In this case the English words are evidently based upon the Latin phrase, but this does not disprove an English origin for the poem *Erthe upon Erthe*, since any verses of the kind must ultimately have been based on the idea that man is dust, and the idea itself must have been first presented and have become widely known through such Latin elegiac phrases as *Memento homo quod cinis es et in cinerem reverteris*, or *De terra plasmasti me*, both of which so frequently accompany *Erthe upon Erthe*, or as the above cited

---

[1] Compare with this the text in the Appendix which begins:
    Whanne eorthe hath eorthe wiþ wrong igete—
and in the French version:
    Quant terre auera en terre large terre gayne.

Terram terra tegat. The verse in *MS. Lansdowne* might rather be considered as supplying further proof of the popular tendency to replace such phrases by English verses, expressing the same idea, but themselves English, not Latin in origin, and making the most of the possible word-play. Such word-plays were evidently popular between the thirteenth and fifteenth centuries. Cf. the well-known passage in *Piers Plowman*, c. xxi. 389.

> So lyf shal lyf lete ther lyf hath lyf anyented,
> So that lyf quyte lyf, the olde lawe hit asketh.
> *Ergo*, soule shal soule quyte and synne to synne wende.

In view of this evidence, I am inclined to think that the Latin version in MS. Harl. 913 is the translation, and the English the original, and that the oldest form of *Erthe upon Erthe* which has been preserved is that found in the four lines in MS. Harl. 2253:—

> Erþe toc of erþe erþe wyþ woh &c.

Short riddling stanzas of the kind, based upon the Latin phrases mentioned above, may have been popular in the thirteenth century, and this particular one was evidently known and used by the author of the *Song on the Times*.[1] The writer of the version preserved in MS. Harl. 913 seems to have been a more learned man, acquainted with poems like the Dialogues between *the Soul and the Body*, who elaborated the four lines of MS. Harl. 2253, and perhaps other verses of the same kind, into a poem of seven six-lined stanzas, the additional couplet often introducing a new idea precisely as in the case of the similarly expanded verse-form in MS. Porkington. Either this man or a later transcriber appears to have added the Latin rendering which accompanies the poem, and to have further exercised himself in varying the word-play. Heuser[2] points out that the mistakes in the MS. would support the view that the English text is a copy of an original in another dialect, and it is possible that the Latin version belongs to this MS. alone, since a second poem in the same MS. is accompanied by an unfinished translation into Latin.

This theory as to the origin of the two texts of the **A** version receives further support from the fact that it also accounts most satisfactorily for the development and popularity of the **B** version. Apart from the play on the word *erthe* and the similarity of the

---

[1] See the Appendix, p. 46.   [2] *Die Kildare-Gedichte* (Bonn, 1904).

theme, there is only one point of close verbal connexion between the two versions. In MS. Harl. 913 (A) the sixth stanza runs as follows:—

> Erþ gette on erþ gersom & gold,
> Erþ is þi moder, in erþ is þi mold.
> Erþ uppon erþ be þi soule hold;
> Er erþe go to erþe, bild þi long bold.
> Erþ bilt castles, and erþe bilt toures;
> Whan erþ is on erþe, blak beþ þe boures.

In the **B** version, the rimes *gold* : *mold*, *toures* : *boures*, regularly recur in the third and fourth stanzas, and line 5 of the **A** text is preserved in slightly modified form in the first line of verse 3:—
(MS. Harl. 4486, vv. 3 and 4)

> Erthe apon erthe wynnethe castelles and towres.
> Then seythe erthe to erthe: 'These bythe alle owres.'
> When erthe apon erthe hath byggede vp his bowres,
> Then schalle erthe for the erthe suffre scharpe schowres.
>
> Erthe gothe apon erthe as molde apon molde.
> So goethe erthe apon erthe alle gleterynge in golde,
> Lyke as erthe unto erthe neuer go scholde,
> And ȝet schalle erthe into erthe rather then he wolde.

In the Cambridge text the rime-words *towres* : *bours* are introduced twice over, representing both the versions given above:—

(ll. 63, 64)   Erthe bygyth hallys & erthe bygith towres,
               When erth is layd in erth, blayke is his bours;

as in the **A** version;

(ll. 5, 7)   Erthe vpon erth has hallys & towris ...
             But quan erth vpon erth has bygyd his bowres,

as in the **B** version.

The two stanzas of the **B** version which contain these rime-words are the two which recur most frequently on tombstones and mural inscriptions, and it seems possible that they represent a second early form of the *Erthe* poems. It is evident that the rime-words *gold* : *mold*, *bowres* : *towres*, depend upon an early tradition. Probably verses similar to the short stanza in MS. Harl. 2253, and containing these words, were in existence before the learned writer of the longer **A** text in MS. Harl. 913 introduced them in his poem, and, becoming widely known, formed the nucleus of the **B** version. Both the **A** and the **B** versions might therefore be held to depend upon popular stanzas of this kind, which gave rise about the end of the thirteenth century to the long poem of MS. Harl. 913, and during the fourteenth century to the original of the **B** version, a poem in seven four-lined stanzas. The earlier version is connected more particularly with the Southwest Midland district; the later seems to have originated rather in the North or North Midlands, but it soon became known all over England, and is found in the South of Scotland shortly after 1500. Only one fifteenth-century writer, the author of the Cambridge text, shows direct knowledge of the **A** text, but the **B** version was evidently widely known, and a favourite theme for additions and modifications. On tombstones and mural inscriptions it survived up to the nineteenth century.

Later Versions of the Poem.

As has been already pointed out, the Middle English texts of *Erthe upon Erthe* occur for the most part in the Commonplace Books of the day, often on the spare leaves at the beginning or end of the MS., as if the collector or some later owner had been struck by the poem and anxious to preserve it. That this interest was not confined to the fifteenth century is shown by the occurrence of the text in the Maitland and Reidpeth MSS. A still later instance of it occurs in the Pillerton Hersey Registers, dating from 1559 onwards, where the following verse has been scribbled on the last leaf, probably by some seventeenth-century clerk (cf. C. C. Stopes, *Athenaeum*, Sept. 19, 1908):—

> Earth upon earth bould house and bowrs,
> Earth upon earth sayes all is ours.
> Earth upon earth when all is wroght,
> Earth upon earth sayes all is for nought.

Here the first two lines represent a corrupt type of the same lines in verse 3 of the **B** version, while the rimes *wroght* : *nought* recall verse 1.

Another interesting trace of a late popular version is mentioned in the *Gentleman's Magazine* for March, 1824, where a certain Mr. J. Lawrence tells how he was invited, during a visit to Beaumont Hall, Essex, to see the following inscription, written and decorated by a cow-boy on an attic wall:—

> Earth goes upon the earth, glittering like gold;
> Earth goes to the earth sooner than 'twould;

Earth built upon the earth castles and towres;
Earth said to the earth, 'All shall be ours.'

Here portions of verses 3 and 4 of the **B** version have been combined as in the epitaphs at Melrose and Clerkenwell cited below, pointing either to a corrupt popular version of the **B** text, or possibly to an earlier type[1] in which the rimes *gold* : *mold*, &c. were immediately associated with the rimes *towres* : *bowres* as in **A** (MS. Harl. 913, v. 6). The former assumption is the more probable, since the verse appears to be directly based upon stanzas 3 and 4 of the usual **B** version.

The majority of the later instances of the text occur on tombstones or memorial tablets. The poem was peculiarly adapted for this purpose, based as it was on the very words of the Burial Service. Indeed, the short verses from which it is here assumed to have originated might well be supposed to have been written in the first place as epitaphs, if evidence of the use of English epitaphs in the thirteenth century[2] were forthcoming. As has been already stated, the seven verses of the normal **B** version occurred in full among the mural paintings in the Chapel of the Holy Trinity at Stratford-on-Avon, belonging to the Guild of the Holy Cross, where they appear to have been used as a monumental inscription already in the latter part of the fifteenth century.

A well-known late instance of the text is the inscription on a tombstone in the parish churchyard which surrounds Melrose Abbey, mentioned by Scott. The stone is headed as follows:—

Memento Mori.
Here lyes James Ramsay, portioner of Melrose, who died July 15th, 1761.

On the back is the following verse:—

The Earth goeth on the Earth
  Glistring like gold,
The Earth goeth to the Earth
  Sooner than it wold;
The Earth builds on the Earth
  Castles & Towers,
The Earth says to the Earth:
  'All shall be ours.'

---

[1] See p. xxxiv above.
[2] The earliest known epitaphs in English date from the fourteenth century.

This was translated into German by Theodor Fontane (*Poems*, 4th edit., Berlin, 1892, p. 447). Cf. Fiedler, *Mod. Lang. Review*, April 1908.

Other inscriptions are as follows:—

On an old brass, quoted by W. Williams, *Notes and Queries*, I. vii. 577, and thought by him to belong to the Church of St. Helen's, London [1]:—

> 'Here lyeth ye bodyes of
> James Pomley, ye sonne of ould
> Dominick Pomley and Jane his
> wyfe: ye said James deceased ye 7th
> day of Januarie Anno Domini 1592
> he beyng of ye age of 88 years, &
> ye sayd Jane deceased y^e — day
> of — D —
>
> Earth goeth upō Earth as moulde upō moulde;
> Earth goeth upō Earth all glittering as golde,
> As though earth to ye earth never turne sholde;
> And yet shall earth to ye earth sooner than he wolde.

On a tomb at Edmonton of unknown date (possibly sixteenth century), mentioned by Weever (*Ancient Funerall Monuments*) in 1631, and by Pettigrew (*Chronicles of the Tombs*, p. 67) in 1857:—

> Erth goyth upon erth as mold upon mold,
> Erth goyth upon erth al glisteryng in gold,
> As though erth to erth ner turne shold,
> And yet must erth to erth soner than he wolde.

Formerly on a headstone in St. James's Churchyard, Clerkenwell, deciphered about 1812, but already lost in 1851, probably owing to the dismantling of the churchyard. (Cf. *Notes and Queries*, III. i. 389):—

> Earth walks on Earth like glittering gold;
> Earth says to Earth 'We are but mold'.
> Earth builds on Earth castles & towers;
> Earth says to Earth, 'All shall be ours!'

Formerly on a tombstone at St. Martin's, Ludgate, to Florens

---

[1] There is no record of this brass at the church of St. Helen's, Bishopsgate.

Caldwell esq. of London & Ann Mary Wilde, his wife (Pettigrew, p. 67)[1]:—

> Earth goes to Earth, as mold to mold;
> Earth treads on Earth, glittering in gold:
> Earth as to Earth returne ne'er shoulde;
> Earth shall to Earth goe e'er he wolde.
>   Earth upon Earth consyder may;
>   Earth goes to Earth naked away.
> Earth though on Earth be stowt & gay
> Earth shall from Earth passe poore away.
>   Be mercifull & charitable,
>   Relieve the poor as thou art able.
>   A shrowd to the grave
>   Is all thou shalt have.

This interesting monument has unfortunately disappeared. Doubtless there are many other traces of the poem to be found, but it appears to have been rarely used on tombstones after 1700,[2] and earlier monuments, unless specially preserved, are rarely decipherable at the present day.

Literary Interest.

Erthe upon Erthe cannot be said to possess great literary value in itself. The interest of the poem lies chiefly in its evident popularity, and in the insight it gives into the kind of literature which became popular in the Middle Ages. It belongs essentially to the same class as the *Soul and Body* Poems, and the *Dance of Death*. In the early days of its introduction into Western Europe, Christianity made great use in its appeal to the mass of the people of the fear of death and dread of the Judgement. The early monastic writers dwelt upon the idea of man's mortality and decay, and the transitoriness of human rank and pleasure. Hence the frequency with which such themes as the *Dance of Death* were treated in literature and in art. Closely allied with this idea of the fleeting nature of earthly things, and to some extent a result of it, was the

---

[1] Dated 1590 by Ernest R. Suffling, *Epitaphia* (1909), p. 282.
[2] A late instance of its use is given by Ch. Box (*Elegies and Epitaphs*, Glouc. 1892) as found by him on the tomb of a bricklayer, who died in 1837, aged 90:—

> Earth walks upon Earth like glittering gold,
> Earth says to Earth, 'We are but mould';
> Earth builds upon Earth castles and towers,
> Earth says to Earth, 'All is ours'!

conception of the separation of man's bodily from his spiritual self which pervades all mediaeval post-Christian literature. In Old English times already, this sense of a sharp division between the two is embodied in No. xliv of the O.E. *Riddles*:—

> [1] Ic wat indryhtne æþelum deorne
> ʒiest in ʒeardum, þæm se grimma ne mæg
> hungor sceðða̅n ne se hata þurst,
> yldo ne adle [ne se enga deað],
> ʒif him arlice esne þenað,
> se þe agan sceal [his ʒeongorscipe]
> on þam siðfæte : hy gesunde æt ham
> findaþ witode him wiste 7 blisse,
> cnosles unrim, care, ʒif se esne
> his hlaforde hyreð yfle
> frean on fore, ne wile forht wesan
> broþer oþrum : him þæt bam sceðeð,
> þonne hy from bearme begen hweorfað
> anre magan ellorfuse
> moddor 7 sweostor.

This sets forth the same conception of the duality in man as is represented in the O.E. *Speech of the Soul to the Body*, and in the whole group of *Soul and Body* poems, and the idea recurs constantly in other monastic texts, cf. Morris, *O.E. Miscellany*, iii (*Sinners Beware*), p. 83 :—

> 326. þe feondes heom forþ ledeþ
>   Boþe lychom and saule.
> 331–336. þe saule seyþ to þe lychome,
>   Accursed wurþe þi nome,
>   þin heaued and þin heorte.
>   þu vs hauest iwroht þes schome,
>   And alle þene eche grome
>   Vs schall euer smerte.

MS. Harl. 2253, fol. 106, vº, l. 7 : þe fleysh stont aʒeyn þe gost. These two fundamental ideas of the transitoriness and hence

---

[1] Printed from Grein-Wülcker, *Bibliothek der ags. Poesie*, iii. 212.—(I know of a most noble guest in the dwellings, hidden from men, whom fierce hunger cannot torment, nor burning thirst, nor age, nor sickness [nor close-pressing death], if the servant who shall [bear him company] in his course serves him honourably: they, prospering, shall find abundance and bliss, countless joys, allotted to them at home, but (they shall find) sorrow, if the servant obeys his lord and master ill upon their journey, and will not show him reverence, the one brother to the other: that shall afflict them both, when they two depart, hastening hence, from the bosom of their common kinswoman, mother and sister.)

worthlessness of man's earthly part, and the cleavage between it and his spiritual part, lie at the root of much of the mediaeval literature, and represent the two not incompatible extremes to which the monastic ideal of life, from its very one-sidedness, was capable of leading: on the one hand a certain morbid materialism, on the other an ascetic mysticism. Nor can it be denied that the mediaeval mind took a certain grim pleasure in dwelling upon the more grotesque aspect of these things. The O.E. poet found the same enjoyment in describing his 'Ᵹifer'—

> [1] se wyrm, þe þa ȝeaȝlas beoð
> nædle scearpran: se genydeð to
> ærest eallra on þam eorðscɪæfe,

as the painters of the *Dance of Death* in the drawing of their skeletons and emblems of mortality, or the Gothic carver in his gargoyles. Perhaps, too, some satisfaction in dwelling upon the hollowness of earthly joys, and the bitter fate of those who took their fill of them, was not lacking to a few of those who had turned their backs upon them.

Erthe upon Erthe is perhaps more especially concerned with the first of the two conceptions mentioned above, man's mortality, but, as has already been shown, a close connexion exists between it and the *Soul and Body* poems, and though the idea of the duality in man is not mentioned, it is certainly present. The poem is more popular in form than either the *Dance of Death* or the various *Soul and Body* Dialogues, perhaps because of its purely English origin, and seems to represent a later and more popular product of the ideas which gave rise to the other two groups. Its short mono-rimed stanza, its jingling internal rime, and its half-riddling, half-punning character, appear to have especially commended it to popular favour, and it is significant that it became most widely-known in its simpler forms.

---

[1] Grein-Wülcker, iii. 105.—(The worm whose jaws are sharper than needles, who first of all the worms in the grave forces his way to him.)

Editor's Note.

In preparing the text of this edition, all the available MSS. have been consulted, the only two not examined being William Billyng's MS. and the Brighton MS., which were formerly in the possession of private owners, and have eluded all search for them. As exhaustive a search as was possible has been made for other texts of the poem, but it has often escaped cataloguing, and it is probable that other copies of the **B** version, at least, exist.

The punctuation, inverted commas,. and regular use of initial capitals in the text are the Editor's. The MSS. vary in their use of capitals, the same MS. being often inconsistent with itself, while the Cambridge text frequently employs them for unimportant words in the middle of the line, as p. 33, l. 45, Ar, &c. Capitals have been added in the case of all proper names. Letters and words which are obscure or illegible in the MS., or which appear to have been accidentally omitted, are enclosed in square brackets, and a hyphen has been inserted where the MS. separates a prefix or particle from the rest of the word. The MS. writings ff, þ, 3, v for u and vice versa, have been retained in the text, and ll̄, t̄h, expanded to lle, the, but it was not thought advisable to expand m̄, n̄, to me, ne, nor other letters such as d, r, g, when written with a final flourish. Fifteenth-century scribes appear to have used such flourishes at the end of the word rather as a matter of habit than with any particular meaning, and the forms to which expansion of them would lead, such as *one*, *onne* for *on*, are frequently most improbable. It was therefore thought better to ignore such flourishes, or to indicate the persistent use of them by a footnote.

As the conclusions arrived at in the Introduction with regard to the relationship of the English and Latin versions in MS. Harl. 913, and the verbal connexion with the *Soul and Body* Dialogues, agree, to some extent, with those indicated by Heuser, *Die Kildare-Gedichte*, pp. 176-80, it is only reasonable to state that the greater part of the work upon the subject had been done, and a projected article upon it written in reply to Professor Fiedler's in the *Modern Language Review*, before I had any knowledge of Heuser's text, and that my conclusions had been formed independently of his, though his have helped to strengthen and confirm them. Moreover I owe his work a very real debt, since I first learned from it of the existence of the Cambridge Text, which has been a most important link in the building up of the general theory as to the connexion between the different versions of the poem.

In conclusion, it is a pleasure to express thanks for kind and courteous assistance to the authorities of the British Museum, the Public Record Office, the Bodleian, Cambridge University Library and Lincoln Cathedral Library; to the librarian of Lambeth Palace Library, to whom I am indebted for the collation of the Lambeth text; to the authorities of Magdalene College, Cambridge, for permission to copy and print the Maitland text; to Lord Harlech for the loan of the Porkington MS.; to Professor Fiedler for permission to use the Brighton text; to Professor Priebsch, who pointed out the text in MS. Harl. 4486; to Miss Helen Sandison, of Bryn Mawr College, U.S.A., for the discovery of the text in the Appendix and for two of the Analogues, and to Professor Skeat for valuable advice and suggestions. In particular this text owes much to my Father, Sir James Murray of the *Oxford Dictionary*, who has read the proofs, and in the midst of his own arduous work has always been ready with help and advice, to my friend Miss K. S. Block, Lecturer in English at the Royal Holloway College, and, above all, to Dr. Furnivall, in whom all scholars and students of English mourn to-day the loss of a great pioneer, and an ever-ready friend and adviser.

OXFORD,
July 1910.

Since this was sent to press two other copies of the **B** version have come to light at Cambridge, and have by kind permission been inserted on pp. 47, 48 as Appendix II:—

(**B** 19) MS. Trinity College R. 3. 21, fol. 33, v°, a copy of the normal **B** version in seven stanzas.

(**B** 20) MS. Trinity College B. 15. 39, fol. 170, which contains nine stanzas of the expanded text preserved in MSS. Lambeth and Laud, and appears to represent a distinct copy of the original of these two (see Introd. p. **xix**).

THE MIDDLE ENGLISH POEM
ERTHE UPON ERTHE.

I.

A VERSION.

1.

MS. HARLEIAN 2253. c. 1307.   [fol. 57, v⁰.]

Erþe toc of erþe erþe wyþ woh,
Erþe oþer erþe to þe erþe droh,
Erþe leyde erþe in erþene þroh,
Þo heuede erþe of erþe erþe ynoh.   4

2.

MS. HARLEIAN 913. c. 1308–1330.   [fol. 62, r⁰.]

1   [1]Whan erþ haþ erþ iwonne wiþ wow,
Þan erþ mai of erþ nim hir inow.
Erþ vp[2] erþ falliþ fol frow[3];
Erþ toward erþ delful him drow.   4
Of erþ þou were makid, and mon þou art ilich;
In on erþ awaked þe pore and þe riche.

Terram per iniuriam cum terra lucratur,
Tunc de terra cepiam[4] terra sorciatur.   8
Terra super aream subito frustratur;   [fol. 62, v⁰.]
Se traxit ad aridam terraque tristatur.
De terra plasmaris, es similis[5] virroni,
Vna terra pauperes ac dites sunt proni.   12

---

[1] Cf. *Reliquiae Antiquae*, II. 216; Furnivall, *Early Eng. Poems and Lives of Saints*, p. 150; Heuser, *Kildare-Gedichte*, p. 180.   [2] read upon.
[3] *in margin* festine.   [4] MS. cepiam, so *Reliq. Ant.*; Furn., Heuser, copiam.
[5] MS. simil', Furn. simile.

B

(*MS. Harleian* 913.)

2   Erþ geþ on erþ wrikkend in weden,
     Erþ toward erþ wormes to feden ;
     Erþ berriþ[1] to erþ al is lif deden ;
     When erþ is in erþe, heo muntid[2] þi meden.   16
When erþ is in erþe, þe rof is on þe chynne[3] ;
Þan schullen an hundred wormes wroten on þe skin.

    Vesta pergit uestibus super uestem vare,
    Artatur & uermibus vesta pastum dare ;   20
    Ac cum gestis omnibus ad uestam migrare ;
    Cum uesta sit scrobibus, quis wlt[4] suspirare ?
Cum sit uesta ponita[5], doma tangit mentum ;
Tunc in cute candida verrunt[6] uermes centum.   24

3   Erþ askiþ erþ, and erþ hir answerid,
     Whi erþ hatid erþ, and erþ erþ verrid.
     Erþ haþ erþ, and erþ erþ teriþ,
     Erþ geeþ on erþ, and erþ erþ berriþ.   28
Of erþ þow were bigun, on erþ þou schalt end ;
Al þat þou in erþ wonne[7], to erþ schal hit wend.

    Humus humum repetit, & responsum datur,
    Humum quare negligit, & humo fruatur.   32
    Humus humum porrigit, sic & operatur,
    Super humum peragit, humo quod[8] portatur.
Humo sic inciperis, ac humo meabis ;
Quod humo quesieris, humo totum dabis.   36

4   Erþ get hit[9] on erþ maistri and miȝte ;   [fol. 63, 1º.]
     Al we beþ erþ, to erþ we beþ idiȝte ;
     Erþ askeþ carayne of king and of kniȝt ;
     Whan erþ is in erþ, so lowȝ he be liȝt.   40
Whan þi riȝt and þi wowȝ wendiþ þe bi-for,
Be þou þre niȝt in a þrouȝ, þi frendschip is i-lor.

---

[1] *MS.* b'riþ, *Furn., Reliq. Ant.* beriþ, *Heuser* berriþ, cf. l. 28.   [2] muntiþ, *in margin* metitur.   [3] *MS. originally* schynne, s *erased*.   [4] vult, *cf. Furn.*   [5] *MS.* pōita, *Furn., Heuser* posita.   [6] *in margin* trahunt.   [7] *in margin* lucrataris, *Heuser* lucrabaris.   [8] *MS.* humo q, *Reliq. Ant., Furn.* humoque, *Heuser* humo quod.   [9] ? getith, *in margin* lucratur.

(*MS. Harleian* 913.)

Terra uimque¹ brauivm terra collucratur;
Totus cetus hominvm de terra patratur²; 44
Ops cadauer militvm que regis scrutatur;
Cum detur in tumulvm, mox terra voratur.
Cum ius & iusticivm coram te migrabunt,
Pauci per trinoctivm mortem deplorabunt. 48

5 Erþ is a palfrei to king and to quene,
Erþ is ar³ lang wei, þouw we lutil wene,
Þat weriþ grouer and groy⁴ and schrud so schene,
Whan erþ makiþ is liuerei, he grauiþ vs in grene. 52
Whan erþ haþ erþ wiþ streinþ þus geten,
Alast he haþ is leinþ miseislich i-meten.

Dic uestam⁵ dextrarium regique regine,
Iter longum marium, quod est sine fine, 56
Indumentum uarium dans cedit sentine⁶,
Quando⁷ dat corrodium, nos tradit ruine.
Cum per fortitudinem tenet hanc lucratam,
Capit longitudinem misere metatam. 60

6 Erþ gette on erþ gersom and gold,
Erþ is þi moder, in erþ is þi mold.
Erþ uppon erþ be þi soule hold;
Er erþe go to erþe, bild þi long bold. 64
Erþ bilt⁸ castles, and erþe bilt toures; [fol. 63, v°.]
Whan erþ is on erþe, blak beþ þe boures.

Humus querit plurima super humum bona,
Humus est mater tua, in qua sumas dona⁹. 68
Anime sis famula super humum prona;
Domum dei perpetra mundo cum corona.
Ops turres edificat ac castra de petra;
Quando¹⁰ fatum capiat, penora sunt tetra. 72

---

¹ *MS.* uīqʒ, *Reliq. Ant.*, *Furn.* vincit, *Heuser* vimque.   ² *MS.* pᵃrtratur, *Furn.* portratur.   ³ *MS.* ar, *Heuser* a.   ⁴ *Heuser* grey (*lies* fou and grey?).   ⁵ *Furn.* est tam.   ⁶ *MS.* eōtine, *Furn.* sentine, *Reliq. Ant.* sentinæ, *so* reginæ, ruinæ.   ⁷ *MS.* Qn̄, *Furn.* omne.   ⁸ *in margin* bildiþ.   ⁹ *Furn.* H. dorna.   ¹⁰ *MS.* qn̄, *Furn.* quin *or* quando.

(*MS. Harleian* 913.)

7 Þenk man in lond[1] on þi last ende,
   Whar of þou com and whoder schaltou wend.
   Make þe wel at on wiþ him þat is so hend,
   And dred þe of þe dome lest sin þe schend.   76
For he is[2] king of blis, and mon of moche mede,
Þat deliþ þe dai fram niȝt, and leniþ lif and dede.

   De fine nouissimo mauors mediteris,
   Huc quo ueneris uico, dic quo gradieris.   80
   Miti prudentissimo concordare deris,
   Hesides iudic[i]o[3], ne noxa dampneris.
Quia rex est glorie, dans mensura restat;
Mutat noctem de die, vitam mortem prestat.   84
                              Amen.

---

[1] *Heuser* ? ilome.   [2] *MS.* hᵉis.   [3] *MS.* iudico : *Reliq. Ant.* judicio, *Furn., Heuser* iudicio.

II

B VERSION.

1.

WILLIAM BILLYNG'S MS. c. 1400–1430 ?.

1. [1]Erth owte of erth is wondyrly wroght,
Ffor erth hath geten of erth a nobul thyng of noght,
Erthe uppon erthe hath set alle hys thoght
How erthe uppon erthe may be hygh broght.   4

2. Erthe uppon erthe yet wolde be a kynge,
But how erth shall to erth thynketh he nothyng;
But when erth byddyth erth his dute hom bryng,
Than shall erth fro erth have a peteus[2] partyng.   8

3. Erth wynnyth uppon erth both castellys and towris;
Than sayth erth unto erth : 'This is alle owres'.
But whan erth uppon erth hath byllyd all his bowrys,
Thanne shalle erth for erth suffer sharpe showres.   12

4. Erth byldyth uppon erth as molde uppon molde,
And erth goth uppon erth glyttryng alle gold,
Lyke as erth unto erth neuer goe sholde;   15
Ann justly tha[n][3] shalle erth go to erth rather þan[4] he wolde.

5. Why man erth loveth erth wondyr me thynke,
Or why that erth for erth swet wylle or swynke,
Ffor whan erth uppon erth is broght within þe[5] brynke,
Than shal þe[6] erth of erth have a ryght fowle sty[n]ke[6]. 20

6. Memento[7] homo quod cinis es et in cinerem reverteris.
Ffac bene dum vivis, post morte[m][8] vivere si vis.
Whan lyffe is most louyd and deth most hated,
Than deth drawyth hys drawght and maketh man ful naked. 24

---

[1] *From Bateman's print* (*William Billyng, Fice Wounds of Christ, Manchester*, 1814).   [2] *Bateman* petrus.   [3] *B.* tha.   [4] *B.* yä.
[5] *B.* w^ti y^e.   [6] *B.* y^e; styke.   [7] *B.* momento.   [8] *D.* morte.

2.

MS. THORNTON. c. 1440. [fol. 279.]

Memento homo Quod Sinis Es
Et in cenerem Reuerteris.

1 [1] Erthe owte of erthe es wondirly wroghte,
Erthe hase getyn one erthe a dignyte of noghte,
Erthe appone erthe hase sett alle his thoghte
How þat erthe appone erthe may be heghe broghte.   4

2 Erthe appone erthe wolde be a kynge,
Bot howe þat erthe to erthe sall thynkis he no thynge.
When erthe bredis erthe & his rentis [2] home brynge,
Thane schalle [3] erthe of erthe hafe full harde partynge.   8

3 Erthe appone erthe wynnys castells and towrrys.
Thane saise [4] erthe vnto erthe: 'This es alle owrris'.
When erthe appone erthe hase bigged vp his bourris,
Than schalle erthe for erthe suffire scharpe scowrrys [5].   12

4 Erthe gose appone erthe as golde appone golde,
He that gose appone erthe gleterande as golde,
Lyke als erthe neuer more [6] goo to erthe scholde,
And ȝitt schal erthe vnto erthe ȝa rathere þan he wolde.   16

5 Now why þat erthe luffis erthe wondire me thynke,
Or why þat erthe for erthe scholde oþer swete or swynke,
For when þat erthe appone erthe es broghte within brynke,
Thane schalle erthe of erthe hafe a foulle stynke.   20

Mors Soluit Omnia.

---

[1] (f. G. G. Perry, Religious Poems in Prose and Verse (E. E. T. S. No. xxvi. 1867, p. 95, 1889, p. 96); C. Horstmann, Yorkshire Writers, I. 373.
[2] repeated in MS. rentys.   [3] Perry sall, MS., Horstmann schalle.   [4] perh. sase, MS. indistinct, Perry thus sase.   [5] perh. stourrys as in Perry, but all other texts have schowrys.   [6] MS. more, Perry mare.

3.

MS. SELDEN Supra 53.   c. 1450.   [fol. 159, v⁰.]

1 ¹Erthe apon erthe ys wonderly wroth²,
  Erthe apon erthe hath worschyp of nogth,
  Erthe apon erthe hath set³ al hys thowth
  How erthe apon erth myth be hy browth.   4

2 Erthe apon erth wolde be a kynge;
  How erth schal to þe erth thy[n]k⁴ he no thynge.
  Whan erth bydyth erth hys rent h[om]e⁴ brynge,
  Þan schal erth fro þe erth [haue]⁵ a delful partynge⁶.   8

3 Erth apon erth wyn[nyth ca⁷]stellys *and* towrys;
  Þan seyth erth to þe erth: 'Þose beth al owrys'.
  Whan erth apon erth hath byggyt al hys bowrys⁸,
  Þan schal erth for þe erth suffyr scharpe [s]chowrys⁹.   12

4 Lo erth apon erth consyder þou may
  Þat erth cometh owte of þe erth nakyt alway.
  Þan how scholde erth apon erthe be prowt [or gay]¹⁰
  Whan erth schal to þe erth in so pore aray?   16

5 Erth goth on erth as molde doþe on molde,
  Erth goth on erth glydderande in golde,
  Lyk as erth to erth neuyre go scholde.
  Ȝyt schal erth to þe erth rathyr þan þey wolde.   20

6 I cowsayl erth apon erth þat wykytly hath wroht,
  Whyle erth ys apon erth to turne al hys tho[w]th¹¹.
  Now pray we to God þat al erth wrowth,
  Þat erth owt of erth to blys myth be browth.   24

---

¹ *The poem is in a different hand on the last leaf of the MS., and the writing is much worn and stained, and in many cases barely legible. A few letters have been re-written in black ink by a later hand.*   ² wroht, *cf.* nogtb, thowth, browth, *and similar cases of* th *for* ht *in v.* 6.   ³ *MS. perhaps* iset.   ⁴ *MS. obscure.*   ⁵ *omitted in MS.*   ⁶ partyn *re-written in black ink,* ge *of the original hand still clear.*   ⁷ *MS. stained and illegible; portions of* nyth a *seem to be visible.*   ⁸ bow *in original hand,* rys *re-written in black ink.*   ⁹ *The second hand has re-written* chowrys *ignoring the* s *which is no longer visible.*   ¹⁰ o *and* y *re-written, the rest illegible.*   ¹¹ w *no longer legible.*

4.

MS. EGERTON 1995. c. 1430–1450.   [fol. 55, r⁰.]
(William Gregory's Commonplace-Book.)

Memento homo quod cinis es et in cinerem reuerteris.
Whenne lyfe ys moste louyde, and dethe ys moste hatyde,
Dethe drawythe hys draughte, and makythe man nakyde.

1 Erthe owte of þe erthe ys wounderly wroughte,   4
 Erthe vppon erthe hathe sette hys thoughte
 Howe erthe a-pon erthe may be hy broughte[1].

2 Erthe vppon erthe wolde be a kynge;
 Howe erthe shalle vnto erthe thynkythe he noo thynge.   8
 Whenne erthe byddys erthe hys rentys home brynge,
 Thenne shalle erthe of the erthe haue a pytyus partynge.

3 Erthe a-pon erthe wynnys castellis and towrys;
 Thenne erthe saythe vnto[2] erthe: 'Thys ys alle owrys'.   12
 Whenne erthe a-pon erthe hathe bylde vppe hys bourys,
 Thenne shalle erthe for the erthe suffer sharpe schowrys.

4 Erthe goythe a-pon erthe as molde a-pon molde;
 Erthe gothe a-pon erthe alle gleterynge in golde,   16
 Lyke as erthe vnto erthe neuyr [go][3] scholde,
 And yet shalle erthe vnto erthe rathyr thenne he wolde.

5 Why erthe louythe erthe woundyr I thynke,
 Or why erthe for the erthe swete wylle or swynke,   20
 Ffor whenne erthe a-pon erthe ys broughte withyn brynke,
 Thenne shalle erthe of erthe haue a foule stynke.

6 Loo erthe a-pon erthe consyder þou may
 Howe erthe comythe to erthe nakyd alle day.   24
 Why scholde erthe a-pon erthe goo stowte and gay,
 Syn erthe vnto erthe shalle pas in pore a-ray?

7 I consylle erthe a-pon erthe þat wyckydly hathe wroughte,
 Whyle erthe ys a-pon erthe to turne vppe hys thoughte,   28
 And pray to God a-pon erthe that alle the erthe hathe wroughte,
                   [fol. 55, v⁰.]
 That erthe owte of the erthe to blys may be brought.
       Amen.   Caue si vis.

---

[1] *The second line is omitted here and in No. 5, where a new line has been added.*   [2] *MS.* vnt.   [3] *Omitted in MS., but required by metre.*

5.

MS. Harleian 1671. 15th century. [fol. 1*, r⁰.]

1 Erthe apon erthe ys waxyne and wroughte,
  And erthe apon erthe hathe ysette alle hys thoughte
  Howe that erthe apon erthe hye myght be broughte,
  But how that erthe scal to the erthe thyngkethe he nohte. 4

2 Erthe apon erthe wolde be a kyng,
  Butte how that erthe schal to erthe thynketh he no thynge,
  Ffor when erthe byddythe erthe hys rente home¹ brynge,
  Than hathe erthe apon erthe heuy partyng. 8

3 Eerthe apon erthe wynnyth castells and touris,
  And erthe saythe to the erthe : 'Thys ys alle ourys'.
  Wanne erthe apon erthe syttythe wyth-in hys bovrys,
  Yeȝt schalle erthe² for the erthe suffre scharpe schourys. 12

4 Erthe goythe on erthe as mowlde aponne mowlde,
  And erthe goyth on erthe gletterant as golde,
  Like as erthe apon erthe neuer dye schoulde.
  Ȝyt schall erthe to the erthe rather than he wolde. 16

5 Why that erthe louyth erthe wonder me thynke,
  Or why that erthe apon erthe swete or swynke,
  Ffor whanne erthe apon erthe ys brought wyth-in the brynke,
  Than ys erthe apon erthe botte a fowle stynke. 20

6 Erthe apon erthe knowethe eche day
  Howe erthe cometh to the erthe naked alle waye.
  Why schulde erthe apon erthe go stowte or gay,
  Syth erthe apon erthe schal passe in pore aray ? 24

7 I cowncelle erthe apon erthe that wonderly hath wroughte
  Whyles that erthe ys apon erthe to turne all hys thoughte,
  And y pray to God apon erthe that alle erthe hath wroughte,
  That erthe out of erthe to blysse may be broughte. Amen. 28

    ³ Whanne lyf ys moste louyd,
      And dethe ys most hatyd,
      Dethe drawyth hys drawghte
      And maketh a man ful naked. 32
      De terra plasmasti me.

---

¹ *MS.* hime *crossed out, and* home *written in same line.*   ² *MS.* erhte.
³ *written parallel with the poem in the right-hand column. A signature apparently follows, but is indecipherable.*

6.

MS. BRIGHTON. 15th century. [fol. 90, v⁰.]

1 ¹Erthe oute of erthe is wondyrly wroghte,
　Erthe vpon erthe gete nobley of noughte,
　Erthe vpon erthe has sete all his thovghte
　How erthe vpon erthe may be hye brovghte.　　4

2 Erthe vpon erthe wolde be a kynge,
　How erthe sall to erthe thenkys he nothyng,
　For whan erthe byddes erthe his rent home brynge,
　Þan sall erthe from erthe haf petus partynge.　　8

3 Erthe vpon erthe wynnes castells and tours ;
　Than says erthe vnto erthe : 'This is all ovres'.
　But whan erthe opon erthe has bigged his borowes,
　Than sall erthe for the erthe sofur sharpe shovres.　　12

4 Erthe gothe vpon erthe os movlde opon movlde,
　Erthe gothe opon erthe glyderyng os golde,
　Lyke as erthe to erthe neuer go shulde.
　Ʒyte shall erthe to erthe rather þan he wolde.　　16

5 Why þat erthe loues erthe wonder me thynkes,
　Vr why þat erthe vpon erthe swetys or swynkes,
　Ffor whan erthe opon erthe is brente within þe brynkes,
　Þan sall erthe of the erthe hafe a foule stynke.　　20

6 Lo erthe vpon erthe consider þou may
　How erthe comes into þe erthe nakyd all way.
　Why sulde erthe vpon erthe go stovte or gay,
　Sethen erthe oute of erthe sall passe in por aray ?　　24

7 I concell erthe opon erthe þat wykkydly has wrouthe,
　The whyle þat erthe is vpon erthe to turn vp his thouthe,
　And praye to God vpon erthe þat all the erthe wrouhte,
　Þat erthe oute of erthe to blys may be browthe.　　28

---

¹ *Printed, by kind permission, from H. G. Fiedler's text* (*Mod. Lang. Review*, III. iii. 219).

7.

STRATFORD-ON-AVON INSCRIPTION. 15th century.
(Formerly in the Chapel of the Trinity.)

1 Erthe oute of erth ys wondurly wroght,
Erth hath gotyn vppon erth a dygnyte of noght,
Erth ypon erth hath sett¹ all hys thowht
How erth apon erth may be hey browght.   4

2 Erth vpon erth wold be a kyng,
But how that erth gott to erth he thyngkys² nothyng.
When erth byddys erth hys rentys whom bryng,
Then schall erth apon erth haue a hard partyng³.   8

3 Erth apon erth wynnys castellys and towrys;
Then seth erth vnto erth: 'Thys ys all owrys'.
When erth apon erth hath bylde hye⁴ bowrys,
Then schall erth for erth suffur many hard schowrys.   12

4 Erth goth apon erth as man apon mowld,
Lyke as erth apon erth neuer⁵ goo schold.
Erth goth apon erth as glisteryng gold,
And yet schall erth vnto erth rather then he wold.   16

5 Why that erth loueth erth wondur me thynke,
Or why that erth wold for erth other swett or swynke.
When erth apon erth ys broght withyn the brynke,
Then schall erth apon erth have a fowll stynke.   20

6 Lo erth on erth, consedur thow may
How erth commyth to erth nakyd all way.
Why schall erth apon erth goo stowte or gay,
Seth erth out of erth schall passe yn poor aray?   24

7 I counsill erth apone erth that ys wondurly wrogt,
The whyll⁶ þat erth ys apon erthe to torne hys thowht,
And pray to God vpon erth þat all erth wroght,
That all crystyn soullys to þe⁷ blis may be broght.   28

---

¹ *Fisher* (Facsimile of inscription) seth; *Reeves* (Mod. Lang. Notes, ix. 4, 203) sett.   ² *Reeves* thynkys.   ³ *Fisher, Reeves* ptyng.   ⁴ *Fisher* hye, *Reeves* hys; cf. H. 4486 hath bygged hy his bowres.   ⁵ *Fisher* neuu.
⁶ *Fisher, Reeves* wʰyll.   ⁷ *Fisher* y for yᵉ.

8.

MS. RAWLINSON C. 307.   c. 1460.   [fol. 2, r⁰.]

Memento homo quod cinis es et in cinerem reuerteris.

1   Erthe opon erthe hath set alle his thoght,
How that erthe opon erthe may be hy broght.
Erthe oute of erthe is wonderly wroght,
Erthe hase of erthe a dignytie of noght.   4

2   Erthe opon erthe wolde be a kyng,
Bot how erthe shalle to erthe thynkis he nothyng.
Ya bot when erthe byddis erthe his rentis hym bryng,
Than shalle erthe hafe of erthe a fulle harde partyng.   8

3   Erthe opon erthe byggis castels and towres,
Than sais erthe vnto erthe : 'Alle þis is ours'.
Ya bot when erthe opon erthe hath byggid vp his bowres,
Than shalle erthe.[1] for erthe suffre sharpe showres.   12

4   Erthe gose on erthe [1] glitterand as golde,
Like as erthe [1] vnto erthe [1] neuer go shulde.
Ya bot when erthe goeth on erthe as colde opon colde,
Yit shalle erthe vnto erthe rather þanne he wolde.   16

5   Whi that erthe luffis erthe wondre me thynke,
Or whi þat erthe for erthe swete wylle or swynke,
Ffor when erthe [1] opon erthe is brought with-in brynke,
Than shalle erthe hafe of erthe [1] a wonder foule stynke.   20

6   What may erthe say to erthe at beste tyme of alle?
Noght bot þat erthe opon erthe shalle hafe a falle.
Bot when erthe oute of erthe [1] shalle com to the laste calle,
Than salle erthe be [2] fulle ferde for þe sely salle.   24

7   Beholde þou erthe opon erthe what worship þou hase,
And thynk þou erthe opon erthe what maistres þou mase,
And how erthe opon erthe what gatis at þou gase,
And þou salle fynde it forsuthe that þou haste many fase.   28

8   Now he þat erthe opon erthe ordande [3] to go
Graunte þat erthe vpon erthe may govern hym so,
Þat when erthe vnto erthe shalle be taken to,
That þe saule of þis erthe suffre no wo.   32

Final n *is often written* ñ; *so* m̄.   [1] *possibly MS.* ertha; *final* e *in this MS. is often written very like* a.   [2] *looks like* ba.   [3] *looks like* ordanda.

9.

MS. HARLEIAN 4486. 15th century. [fol. 146, r⁰.]

Memento homo quod cinis es & [in] cinerem reuerteris,
Ffac bene dum viuis, post mortem viuere si vis.
When[1] lyffe is most loued[1], & deth is moste hated,
Then dethe[2] drawethe his drawghte & makythe man fulle naked.   4

1 Erthe owte of erthe is wonderly wrowghte,
   Erthe of the erthe hathe gete an abbey of nawte,
   Erthe apon erthe hathe sett alle his thowghte
   How erthe apon erthe may be hye browte.   8

2 Erthe apon erthe be he[3] a kynge,
   Butt how erthe schalle to erthe thynkethe he nothynge.
   [4] When erthe byddethe erthe his rent home brynge,
   Then schalle erthe owte of erthe haue a pyteous partynge.   12

3 Erthe apon erthe wynnethe castelles & towres.
   Then seythe erthe to erthe: 'These bythe alle owres'.
   When erthe apon erthe hath byggede vp his bowres,
   Then schalle erthe for the erthe suffre scharpe schowres.   16

4 Erthe gothe apon erthe as molde apon molde.
   So goethe erthe apon erthe alle gleterynge in golde,
   Lyke as erthe into erthe neuer go scholde,
   And ȝet schalle erthe into erthe rather then he wolde.   20

5 Why erthe louethe erthe wonder me thynke,
   Or why that erthe for erthe swete wylle or swynke,
   Ffor whan erthe apon erthe is browte withyn þe brynke,
   Then schalle erthe of the erthe haue a fowle stynke.   24

6 Loo, erthe apon erthe, consydere thow may
   How erthe commythe to erthe naked alle way.
   Why scholde erthe apon erthe go stowte or gay,
   Whan erthe schalle passe owte of erthe in a pore aray?   28

   [fol. 146, v⁰.]

7 Therfor erthe apon erthe that wykedly hast wroughte,
   Whyle erthe is apon erthe torne agayne thy thowghte,
   And pray to God apon erthe that alle erthe hath wroughte
   That this erthe apon this erthe to blysse may be browte.   32

---

[1] *Final* n *is uniformly written* ñ *in this text excepting in the word* in. *Final* d *is frequently written* d̃.   [2,3] *added above the line.*   [4] *The first words in ll.* 11, 14, 15 *seem to have been freshened up.*

(*MS. Harleian* 4486.)

8 Now Lorde that madyst for erthe & sufferdyst paynes ylle,
Lett neuer this erthe for this erthe in myschyffe spylle,
But that this erthe in this erthe be euer worchynge thy wylle,
So that this erthe fro þis erthe may stye vp to thy hylle.   36

                                               Amen.

10.

MS. LAMBETH 853. c. 1430–1450.   [fol. 35.]

Whanne liif is moost loued, and deeþ is moost hatid:
Þanne dooþ deeþ drawe his drawȝt, & makiþ man ful nakid.
      De terra plasmasti me, &c.

1 Erþe out of erþe is wondirly wrouȝt,   4
Erþe of erþe haþ gete a dignyte of nouȝt,
Erþe upon erþe haþ sett al his þouȝt,
How þat erþe upon erþe may be hiȝ brouȝt.

2 Erþe upon erþe wold he be a king;   8
But how erþe schal to erþe þenkiþ he no [fol. 36] þing;
Whanne þat erþe biddiþ erþe hise rentis hom bring,
Þan schal erþe out of erþe haue a piteuous parting.

3 Erþe vpon erþe wynneþ castels & touris,   12
Þan seiþ erþe to erþe : 'Now is þis al houris'.
Whanne erþe upon erþe haþ biggid up hise boure[s],
Þanne schal erþe upon erþe suffir scharpe schouris.

4 Erþe gooth vpon erþe as molde upon molde,   16
So gooth erþe upon erþe al gliteringe in golde,
Like as erþe vnto erþe neuere go schulde,
And ȝit schal erþe vnto erthe raþer þan he wolde.

ERTHE UPON ERTHE.—B VERSION.

(*MS. Lambeth* 853.)

5 O þou wrecchid erþe þat on erþe traueilist nyȝt and day,   20
   To florische þe erþe, to peynte þe erþe with wantowne aray,
   Ȝit schal þou erþe for al þi erþe, make þou it neuere so queynte & gay,
   Out of þis erþe in-to þe erþe, þere to clinge as a clot of clay. [fol. 37.]

6 O wrecchid man whi art þou proud, þat art of þe erþe makid? 24
   Hider brouȝttist þou no schroud, but poore come þou and nakid.
   Whanne þi soule is went out, & þi bodi in erþe rakid,
   Þan þi bodi þat was rank & undeuout, of alle men is bihatid.

7 Out of þis erþe cam to þis erþe þis wrecchid garnement;   28
   To hide þis erþe, to happe þis erþe, to him was cloþinge lente;
   Now gooþ erþe upon erþe, ruli raggid and rent,
   Þerfore schal erþe vndir þe erþe haue hidiose turment.

8 Whi þat erþe to myche loueþ erþe wondir me þink,   32
   Or whi þat erþe for superflue erþe to sore sweete wole or swynk;
   Ffor whanne þat erþe upon erþe is brouȝt withinne þe brink,
   Þan schal erþe of þe erþe haue a rewful swynk.

9 Lo erþe upon erþe considere þou may,   36
   How erþe comeþ into erþe nakid al way,   [fol. 38.]
   Whi schulde erþe upon erþe go now so stoute or gay,
   Whanne erþe schal passe out of erþe in so poore aray?

10 Wolde God þerfore þis erþe, while þat he is upon this erþe,
    Vpon þis wolde hertili þinke,   40
   & how þe erþe out of þe erþe schal haue his aȝen-risynge,
   And þis erþe for þis erþe schal ȝeelde streite rekenyng;
   Schulde neuere þan þis erþe for þis erþe mysplese heuene king.

11 Þerfore þou erþe upon erþe þat so wickidli hast wrouȝt,   44
    While þat þou erþe art upon erþe turne aȝen þi þouȝt,
    And praie to þat God upon erþe þat al þe erþe haþ wrouȝt,
    Þat þou erþe upon erþe to blis may be brouȝt.

(*MS. Lambeth* 853.)

12 O þou Lord þat madist þis erþe for þis erþe & suffridist
    heere peynes ille,   48
Lete neuere þis erþe for þis erþe myscheue ne spille,
But þat þis erþe on þis [fol. 39] erþe be euere worchinge þi wille,
So þat þis erþe from þis erþe may stie up to þin hiȝ hille.
                                                          Amen.

Memento homo quod cinis es, et in cinerem reuerteris,   52
Ffac bene dum viuis. post mortem viuere si uis.
Tangere qui gaudet. meretricem qualiter audet.
Palmis pollutis. regem tractare salutis.
Credo in deum patrem omnipotentem.   56

    (*Here follows the Creed in English verse.*)

11.

MS. Laud Misc. 23.   Before 1450.   [fol. 111, v°.]

Whan lyf is moost louyd & deeþ is moost hatyd:
Thanne deeth drawyth his draut and makith man ful nakid.

1 Erthe out of erthe is wondirly wrouȝt,
  Erthe of the erthe hath gete a dignyte of nowthe,   4
  Erthe vp-on erthe hath set al his thouȝt
  How that erthe vp-on erthe may be hyȝ browth.

2 Erthe vp-on erthe wolde be a kyng;
  But how erthe shal to erthe thinkiþ he no thing;   8
  Whan that erthe biddeth erthe his rentys hoom bring,
  Thanne shal erthe out of the erthe haue a petous partyng.

(*MS. Laud Misc.* 23.)

3 Erthe vp-on erthe wynnyth castellis and towris[1],
    Tha*n*ne seith erthe to erthe: 'This is al owris.'
    Whan erthe vp-on erthe hath biggid alle his bouris,
    Thanne shal erthe for erthe suffre sharp showris.

4 Erthe gooth up-on erthe as moolde vp-on moolde,
    So gooth erthe vp-on erthe al gleteryng in goolde,
    Like as erth*e* vn-to erthe neu*ere* goo[2] shulde;
    Yit shal erthe vnto erþe[3] rather*e* than he wolde.

5 O thou wrecchid erthe, that on the erthe [fol. 112, 2°] traueylist ny3t and day,
    To florissh*e* the erthe, to peynte the erthe wyth wanton*e* a-ray;
    3it shal thow erthe, for alle thyn erthe, make thow it neu*er* so queynt & gay,
    Out of the erthe in-to the erthe, ther to clynge as clot of clay.

6 O wrecchide man whi art thow prude, that art of erthe makid?
    Hidir broutyst thow no shroude, but pore cam thow & nakid.
    Whan thi soule is went out, & thi body in erthe rakid,
    Thanne thi body that was rank and louyd of alle men, is hatyd.

7 Out of the erthe cam to this erthe his wantyng garnement;
    To hyde this erthe, to wrappe this erthe, to him was clothing lent;
    Now gooth erthe up-on erthe, ruly raggid and rent,
    Therfor shal erthe vndir erthe haue hidous turme*n*t.

8 Whi that erthe louyth erthe wondir me thinke,
    Or whi that erthe for erthe swete wole or swinke;
    Ffor whan that erthe up-on the erthe is brou3t wyth-i*n*ne the brinke,
    Thanne shal erthe of the erthe haue a rewfull*e* stinke.

☞ 9 Lo erthe up-on erthe cousider thow may,
    How erthe in-to the erthe comyth nakid al-way,
    Whi shuld erthe vp-on erthe go stout [fol. 112, v°] or gay,
    Wha*n* erthe shal passe out of erthe in a por*e* aray?

---

[1] towris *added in margin by the same hand.*   [2] *MS.* goo ne; ne *crossed out, and marked* ne̜.   [3] vnto erþe *inserted in red above the line.*

(*MS. Laud Misc.* 23.)

10 Wolde therfore this erthe on this erthe, on this hertly thinke,
How that erthe out of the erthe shal haue risynge, 40
And thus erthe for erthe[1] yeelde shal streyt rikenynge,
Shulde neuere erthe for erthe mysplese heuene kyng.

11 Thow erthe up-on erthe, that wickydly hast wrout,
While that erthe is vp-on erthe, turne a-ȝen thi thout, 44
And preye to God vp-on erthe, that alle the erthe hath wrouȝt,
That erthe vp-on erthe to blisse may be brouȝt.

12 Lord God that erthe madist & for the erthe suffiedist peynys ille,
Lete neuere þis erþe[2] for this erthe myscheue ne spille, 48
But that this erthe in this erthe be euere worching thi wille,
So that erthe fro this erthe stye up on thyn hyȝe hille. Amen.
par charite, God it graunte that it so be.

☞ [3]Tangere qui gaudes meretricem qualiter audes[4]. 52
Palmis pollutis regem tractare salutis.

(*The poem* Whi is the wor[l]d belouyd that fals is and veyn, *follows immediately.*)

---

[1] for erthe *repeated and crossed out in red.* [2] þis erþe *added above the line,* erþe *in red.* [3] *In left margin* de sacerdotibus. [4] *in right margin* hoc in decretis.

12.

MS. Cotton Titus A. xxvi. 15th century. [fol. 153, rº.]

1 Erthe oute of erthe is wondirly wroght,
Erthe of þe erthe hathe goten a dyngnyte of noght,
Erthe vpon erthe hathe set alle hys thovght
Houe erthe vpon erthe maye be hyghe broght. 4

2 Erthe vpon erthe wolde be a kyng;
Bot how erthe shalle to erthe thynkethe he nothyng;
Whan that erthe biddethe erthe hys rentis hom to bryng,
Than shalle erthe oute of erthe haue a pytous partyng. 8

3 Whan erthe vpon erthe wynythe casteles & tourys,
Than says erthe to erthe: 'Þys is alle ourys'.
And whan erthe vpon erthe hathe byggid hys bourys,
Than shalle erthe vpon erthe suffer sharpe shoures. 12

4 Erthe gothe vpon erthe as molde vpon molde [1],
So gothe erthe vpon erthe alle glytryng in golde,
Lyke as erthe into erthe never goo sholde;
And yet shal [2] erthe in to erthe rathar then he wolde. 16

[fol. 153, vº.]
5 O thou wreched erthe that on erthe trauayles nyght & daye
To fflorysshe [3] and paynt þe erthe with wanton araye;
Yet sshalle þou, erthe, for alle thy erthe, make þou it neuer so queynt or gaye,
Oute of thys erthe in to erthe to klyng as clot in claye. 20

6 O wrechyd man, why [4] art þou [5] prowde that of erth art maked,
And hyder thou broght no shrowde, bot pore com and nakyd?
Lewe thy syne and lyffe in ryght,
And than shalt thou lyffe in heuyn as a knyght. 24

Final n *is written* n̄ *as a rule in this text, so* m̄.   [1] *MS.* moldee.
[2] *MS.* shal do *or* de, *the second word crossed out.*   [3] *MS.* To fflorysshe þe erthe, *the last two words crossed out, cf. MS. Lambeth,* v. 5; *MS. Rawl. Poet.,* v. 15.   [4] *MS.* why at, at *crossed out.*   [5] *MS.* þᵗ.

13.

MS. Rawlinson Poetical 32. After 1450. [fol. 32, vo.]
A descripture alchimicall of erthe & the nature of man[1].

  Whanne life is most louyd,
  And deth is most hatid,
  Deth drawith his drauȝte
  And makith a man nakid.   4

1 Erthe oute of erthe
 Is wonderly wrouȝte;
 Erthe hath of the erthe
 ƺetyn a dignite of noughte.   8

2 Erthe a-pon erthe
 Hath set alle his thoughte
 How erthe apon erthe
 May be hiere y-broughte.   12

3 Erthe a-pon erthe
 Wolde be made a kyng,
 How erthe schal to eithe
 Thynkyng no thyng.   16

4 Whanne erthe biddith erthe
 That he his rente hom brynge,
 Thanne schal erthe for erthe
 Haue a petous partynge.   20

5 Whanne erthe apon erthe
 Hath billid al his bowris,
 Thanne schalle erthe for erthe
 Suffre ful harde schowris.   24

6 Erthe a-pon erthe   [fol. 33, 1o.]
 Wynnyth castellis and towris.
 Thanne saithe erthe to erthe:
 'This is alle owris'.   28

7 Erthe gothe apon erthe
 As molde a-pon molde,
 Erthe gothe apon erthe
 Gleteryng alle in golde,   32

---
[1] Added in a later hand, probably 16th century.

(*MS. Rawlinson Poetical* 32.)

8 As thouh erthe to erthe
   Neue*r* a-yen go schulde,
   But yit schal erthe to þe erthe
   Rather thanne he wolde.   36

9 Oute of the erthe cam the erthe
   Wantynge his garnament,
   To hide the erthe, to lappe the erthe,
   To hym was clothing y-lent.   40

10 Now goth the erthe apon erthe
   Disgesily ragged and to-rent,
   Therfore schal erthe vnder erthe
   Suffer ful grete turment.   44

11 Whi that erþe loueþ erthe
   Wonder y may thinke,
   Or whi that erthe for the erthe
   Unresonably swete wol or swynke,   48

12 Ffor whanne erthe vnder erthe   [fol. 33, v⁰.]
   Is brouȝte withynne brynke,
   Thanne schal erthe of the erthe
   Haue an oribyll stynke.   52

13 Yif erthe wold of erthe
   Thus hartily haue thynkynge,
   And how erthe out of erthe
   Shal at last haue risynge,   56

14 Thanne schal erthe for erthe
   Yelde riht streite rekenynge,
   Thanne schuld [erthe] for erthe
   Neuer mys-plese heuene kynge.   60

15 Thow wrecchid erthe þat thus for erthe
   Trauelist nyht and day
   To florische the erthe, to paynte the erthe
   With thi wanton array,   64

16 Yit schalt thou erthe for alle thi erthe,
   Make thou neuer so gay,
   Ffor thi erthe in to erthe
   Clynge as clotte in clay.   68

(*MS. Rawlinson Poetical* 32.)

17 Thinke now erthe how thou in erthe
   Goist euer in dethis¹ grace,
   And thanne thou erthe for the erthe
   Shalt neuer stryue ne race.   72

18 Bute for thou erthe with thi erthe   [fol. 34, rº.]
   Hauntist enuye and hate,
   Therefor schal erthe for erthe
   Be excludid from heuene gate.   76

19 Ffowle erthe whi louyst thou erthe
   That is thi dedly foo,
   And bildist on erthe
   As thou schuldist dwelle euer moo?   80

20 But thou erthe forsake the erthe,
   Or that thou hennys goo,
   Vnder erthe for lust of erthe
   Thou schalt haue sorow and woo.   84

21 Whiles erthe may in erthe
   To festis and to drynkis gon,
   Til the be made frome the erthe
   As bare as any bon.   88

22 Thanne if erthe comyth to erthe
   Makyng sorow and mone,
   Thanne saith erthe to the erthe,
   'Thou were a felow, but now art thou none'.   92

23 Thus the erthe queytith the erthe
   That doith to him seruyse,
   Or tristyn on erthe, or plese the erthe
   In any maner wise.   96

24 Therfor thou erthe be ware of erthe   [fol. 34, vº.]
   And thou the wele auyse,
   Lest thou erthe perische for erthe
   By-fore the hihe iustyse.   100

¹ *MS.* deth is.

(*MS. Rawlinson Poetical* 32.)

25 Ffor the erthe was made of erthe
    At the first begynnynge,
    That erthe schuld labour the erthe
    In trowthe and sore swynkynge ;   104

26 But now erthe lyueth in erthe
    With falshode and begilynge,
    Therfor schal erthe for erthe
    Be punsched in payne euerlastynge.   108

27 But erthe forsake the erthe
    And alle his falshede,
    And of the erthe restore the erthe
    Goodis that ben mys-gete,   112

28 Or that erthe be doluyn in erthe
    And vnder fote y-trede,
    Ffor synne of erthe, þat hath do in erthe,
    Fful sore he schalle be bete.   116

29 Drede thou erthe while thou in erthe
    Hast witte & resoune at thi wille,
    That, erthe, for loue of erthe,
    Thi soule thou nougth spille.   120

30 And thou erthe, repente the in erthe   [fol. 35, r⁰.]
    Of alle that thou hast don ille,
    And thanne schalt thou, erthe apon erthe,
    Goddis biddyngis fulfille.   124

31 Lord God that erthe tokist in erthe,
    And suffredist paynes ful stille,
    Late neuer erthe for the erthe
    In dedly synne ne spille,   128

32 But that erthe in this erthe
    Be doynge euer thi wille,
    So that erthe for the erthe
    Stye vp to thi holy hille.   Amen. S. J.   132

14.

MS. PORKINGTON 10.   15th century.   [fol. 79, v°.]

1 [1] Erthe vppon erthe is woundyrely wrouȝte;
Erthe vppon erthe has set al his þouȝte [2]
How erthe vppon erth to erthe schalle be [3] brouȝte; [fol. 80, r°.]
Ther is none vppon erth has hit in þouȝte.[4]   4
                Take hede!
Whoso þinkyse on [5] his ende, ful welle schal he spede.

2 Erth vppon erth wolde be a kynge;
How erth schal to erthe he þinkis no þinge.   8
When erth byddyþ erth his rent whome brynge,
Then schal erth fro þe erth have a harde parttynge,
                With care;
Ffor erth vppon erþe wottis neuer wer þerfor to fare.   12

3 Erth vppon erth wynnis castyllis & tovris.
Then sayþe erth to erth: 'Al þis is ourus'.
When erth vppon erth has bylde al his bovres,
Then schal erth fro þe erth soffyre scharpe schorrys,   16
                Ande smarte.
Man, amende þe betyme, þi lyfe ys but a starte.

4 Erth gose on erth as molde vponne molde,
Lyke as erth to þe erth neuer a-gayne scholde;   20
Erth gose on erth glytteryng in golde [6],
Ȝet shale erth to þe erth, raþer þen he wolde. [fol. 80, v°.]
                Be owris!
Ȝefe þi almis with þi hande.   Trust to no secatovrs.   24

5 Why þat erth louis erþe merwel me þinke,
[7] Or why erth vppon erth wyl swet or swinke,
[7] Ffor when erth vppon erth is brouȝt to þe brynke,
Then schal erth frov þe erth have a fovl stynke   28
                To smele,
Wars þen þe caryon þat lyis in þe fele.

---

[1] Cf. Halliwell, *Early Eng. Misc. in Prose and Verse*, printed for the Warton Club, 1855, p. 39, Fiedler, *Mod. Lang. Review*, III. iii. 225.   [2,4] MS. þouȝte.   [3] MS. bo.   [5] MS. oñ, oñ, throughout.   [6] MS. in I golde.
[7] These two lines are transposed in the MS.

(*MS. Porkington* 10.)

6 Lo, erth vppon erth, consayfe þis þou maye,
  That þou commys frome þe erth nakyde alway[e];
  How schulde erth vppon erth soe[1] prode or gaye,
  Sen[2] erth vnto erth schal pase in symple araye,
       Unclade?
  Cloth þe nakyd whyl þou may, for so Gode þe bade.

7 Erth vppon erth, me þinkyȝ þe ful blynde,
  That on erth ryches to set al[3] þi mynde;
  In þe gospel wryttyne exampul I fynde,
  The pore went to heyuyn, þe rych to hel I fynde,
       Witt skyle:
  The commandmentis of Gode wolde he not fulfyle. [fol. 81, r⁰.]

8 Erth vppon erth, deyle duly thy goode
  To þe pore pepul þat favtt þe þi fovde,
  Ffor þe loue of þi Lorde, þat rent was on þe roode,
  Ande for þi loue on þe crose sched his[4] hart blode,—
       Go rede!—
  Wittovte anny place to reste on his hede.

9 Erth vppon erth, take tent to my steyuyne;
  Whyl þou leuyst, fulfyle þe werkys of mercy vij.
  Loke þou lete, for oode ne for ewyne,
  Ffor þo byne þe werkis þat helpyne vs to heyuyne,
       In haste.
  Tho dedis who so dose þar, hyme neuer be agaste.

10 Erth vppon erth, be þou neuer so gaye,
   Thow moue[5] wende of þis worlde an vnreydy waye;
   Turne þe betyme, whyle þat þou maye,
   Leste it lede þe into hele, to logege þer for[6] ay,
        In pyne;
   Ffor þer is noþer to gett brede, ale, ne wyne.

---

[1] *MS.* soe, *Halliwell* soe, *Fiedler* goe.   [2] *MS.* señ.   [3] *H.* setal.
[4] *H. F.* schedhis.   [5] *MS.* mōu.   [6] *MS.* þ͛for, *H. F.* therefor.

(*MS. Porkington* 10.)

11 Erth vppon erth, Gode ʒeyf þe grace, [fol. 81, vº.]
  Whyle þou leuuyst vppon erth, to purway þe a place
  In heywyn to dweylle, whyl þat þou hast space ;
  That myrthe for to myse it wer a karful case.   64
       Ffor whye ?
  That myrth is withowttyn ende, I tel þe securlye.

12 I concele erth vppon erth þat wykydely has wroʒte,
  Whyl erth is on erth, to torn alle his þovʒte,   68
  Ande pray to Gode vppon erth, þat al made of nov[ʒte]¹,
  That erth owte of erth to blys may be bovʒte²
       Witt myʒthe³,
  Thorow helpe Jhesu Cryst þat was oure ladis byrthe.   72
     Do for þiself.

---

¹ *MS. only* nov *now legible.*   ² *MS.* bovʒte, *Halliwell* bouʒt, *Fiedler* brouʒt.   ³ *MS. Halliwell* myʒthe, *probably erroneous for* myrthe.

15.

MS. BALLIOL 354. Before 1504. [fol. 207, v⁰.]

(Richard Hill's Commonplace-Book.)

1 Erth owt of erth is worldly wrowght,
Erth hath goten oppon erth a dygnite of nowght,
Erth vpon erth hath [1] set all his thowght,
How þat erth vpon erth myght be hye browght. 4

2 Erth vpon erth wold be a kyng,
But how þat erth shall to erth, he thynkith no thyng;
When erth biddith erth his rentes [2] home bryng,
Then shall erth for erth haue a hard partyng. 8

3 Erth vpon erth wynneth castlles [2] & towres,
Then seyth erth vnto erth : 'Þis is all owres';
But when erth vpon erth hath bildyd his bowres,
Than shall erth for erth suffre hard showres. 12

4 Erth vpon erth hath welth vpon molde,
Erth goth vpon erth glydryng all in golde,
Like as he vnto erth neuer torn shuld;
& yet shal erth vnto erth soner than he wold. 16

5 Why þat erth loweth erth, wonder [3] I thynk;
Or why þat erth will for erth swet or swynk;
For whan erth vpon erth is browght within þe brynk,
Than shall erth for erth suffre a fowle stynk. 20

6 As erth vpon erth were þe worthyes ix,
& as erth vpon erth in honour dide shyne;
But erthe liste not to know how þei shuld enclyn,
& þer crownnys leyd in erth, whan deth hath made hys fyne. 24

Cf. Roman Dyboski, E.E.T.S. extra ser. ci (1907), p. 90. [1] D. erron.
hat[h].   [2] D. reads rentes, castlles.   [3] MS. worder.

(*MS. Balliol* 354.)

7 As erth vpon erth, fulle worthy was Josue, [fol. 208, rº.]
   Dauyd þe worthy kyng, Judas Machabe;
   They were but erth vpon erth, non of them thre,
   And so from erth vnto erth þei loste þer dignite. 28

8 Alisander was but erth, þat all the world wan,
   & Ector vpon erth was hold a worthy man,
   & Julius Cesar þat þe empire first be-gan;
   & now, as erth within erth, þei lye pale & wan. 32

9 Arthur was but erth, for all his renown;
   No more was kyng Charlis, ne Godfrey of Bolown;
   But now erth hath torned þer noblenes vpsodown;
   & thus erth goth to erth, by short conclusion. 36

10 Who so rekyn also of William Conquerowre[1],
   Kyng Harry þe first, þat was of knyghthode flowre[1];
   Erth hath closed them ful streytly in his bowre[1];
   Loo, the ende of worthynes! here is no more socowre[1]. 40

11 Now thei þat leve vpon erth, both yong & old,
   Thynk how ye shall to erth, be ye neuer so bold;
   Ye be vnsiker, wheþer it be in hete or cold,
   Like as your brether[2] did beffore, as I haue told. 44

12 Now ye folk þat be here, ye may not long endure,
   But þat ye shall torn to erth, I do you ensure;
   & yf ye lyst of þe trewth to se a playn fugure,
   Go to seynt Powlis, & see þer the portratowre[1]. 48

13 All ys erth, & shall be erth, as it shewith ther,
   [3] Þer-for, or dredfull deth with his dart you dere,
   & for to torn in to erth, no man shall it forbere,
   Wisely purvey you beffore, & þer-of haue no fere. 52

14 Now, sith by deth we shal al pas, it is to vs certeyn,
   For of þe erth we com all, & to þe erth shall torn agayn;
   Þer-for to strive of grucche it were but in vayn,
   For all is erth, & shall be erth, no thyng more certayn. 56

[1] *D. reads* -owr *throughout.*   [2] *D. erron.* brother.   [3] *Line* 50 *would be better placed after l.* 51.

(*MS. Balliol* 354.)

15 Now erth vppon erth, consydre thow may,
How erth commeth to erth nakyd all way.
Why shuld erth vpon erth go stowt or gay,
Sith erth owt of erth shall passe in pore a-ray? 60

16 I consaill you vpon erth þat wikkidly haue wrowght,
Whill þat erth is on erth, torn vp your thowght,
& pray to God vppon erth, þat all þe erth hath wrowght,
Þat erth owt of erth to blis may be browght. 64
   Amen.

16.

MS. HARLEIAN 984. 16th century. [fol. 72, 1º.]

6 [1] How schulde erthe vpon erthe be prud & gay
When erthe schal to erthe in so pore aray?

7 I consell erthe vpon erthe þat wikyd hade wroȝt,
Whyle erthe ys apon erthe to turne al his þoȝt, 4
Ande pray to God þat al þe world wroȝt [2]
Þat erthe out of erthe to blesse may be broȝt.

---

[1] *The previous leaf of the MS., which evidently contained the beginning of the poem, has been torn out.*   [2] *MS.* woȝt.

17.

THE MAITLAND MS. (PEPYSIAN MS. 2553, p. 338.)
c. 1555–1585.

1 [1]Eyrd vpone eird wondirfullie is wrocht,
   Eird hes gottin vpone eird ane dignite for nocht,
   Eird apone eird hes set all his thocht
   How þat[2] eird vpone eird till hicht may be brocht.　　4

2　Eird apone eird wald fayne be a king,
   And how þat eird gois to eird thinkis he no thing.
   Quhone eird byddis eird his rentis hame to bring,
   Than sall eird haue to eird herd depairting.　　8

3　Eird apon eird wynnis castellis and towris,
   Than sayis eird vntill eird : 'All þir ar owris'.
   Quhone eird apone eird hes biggit all his bowris,
   Than sall eird vpone eird suffir scharp schowris.　　12

4　Eyrd apone eird and mold vpone mold,
   Lyke as eird vnto eird never go sold.
   Eird gois apone eird glitterand as gold,
   Ʒit sall eird go to eird sonar nor he wold.　　16

5　How þat eird luiffis eird grit wondir I think,
   Or quhy þat eird will for eird owþir swet or swynk.
   Quhone þat eird within eird is closit vndir bynk,
   Than sall eird within eird haue ane ewill stynk.　　20

6　Lo eird vpone eird considdir þow may,
   How eird vnto[3] eird gois nakit away,
   Quhy sould eird apone eird go ower proud or gay,
   Sen eird vntill eird sall wend in pure array?　　24

7　I counsall eird vpone eird þat wondirlie is wrocht,
   Quhill[4] eird is apone eird to turne all his thocht,
   And pray to God apone eird þat maid all of nocht,
   That eird vpone eird to blys may be brocht.　　28
          Quod marsar.

---

[1] *Printed by kind permission of the authorities of Magdalene College, Cambridge.*　[2] *MS.* yat; þ *regularly written as* y.　[3] *MS.* apone *crossed out,* vnto *written above.*　[4] *MS.* q^{ll}.

18.

JOHN REIDPETH'S MS. CAMBR. UNIV. LIBR. Ll. 5. 10.
[fol. 43, v⁰.]
(Transcribed from the Maitland MS. 1622-3.)

1 Eird vpoun eird wonderfull is wrocht,
Eird hes gottin vpoun eird ane dignitie for nocht,
Eird vpoun eird hes sett all his thocht
How þat[1] eird vpoun eird till hicht may be brocht. 4

2 Eird vpoun Eird wold fane be ane king, [fol. 44, r⁰.]
And how þat eird gois to eird thinkis he nothing.
Quhen eird bidd*is* eird his rentis hame to bring,
Than sall eird haue to eird herd depairting. 8

3 Eird vpoun Eird wins castell*is* and towris;
Than sayis eird vnto eird: 'All now ar ouris'.
Quhen eird vpoun eird hes biggit all his towris,
Than sall eird vpoun eird suffer grit showris. 12

4 Eird vpoun eird and mold vpoun mold,
Lyk as eird vnto eird neuer go sold,
Eird gois vpoun eird glitterand as gold,
Ȝitt sall eird go to eird sonear nor he wald. 16

5 How þat eird luiffis eird grit wonder I think,
Or quhy þat eird will for eird owther sweit or swink,
Quhen þat eird wi*th*in eird is closit vnder bink,
Than sall eird wi*th* eird haue ane evill stink. 20

6 Lo eird vpoun eird considder thow may
How eird vnto eird gois nakit away,
Quhy sould eird vpoun eird go our[2] proud or gay,
Sen eird vntill eird sall wend in pure aray? 24

7 I counsall eird vpoun eird þat wondirlie is wrocht,
Q*uhi*ll eird is vpoun eird to turne all his thocht,
And pray to God vpoun eird þat maid all of nocht,
That eird vpoun eird to blis may be brocht. 28
Quod dumbar.

---

[1] *MS.* yat; þ *regularly written as* y.   [2] over, *MS.* o*r*.

III. THE CAMBRIDGE TEXT.

CAMBRIDGE UNIV. LIBR. Ii. 4. 9. 15th century. [fol. 67, r⁰.]

1 Erthe vpon erth is waxin and wrought,
Erthe takys on erth a nobylay of nought;
Now erthe vpon erthe layes all his þought
How erthe vpon erthe sattys all at noght. 4

2 Erthe vpon erth has hallys & towris[1];
Erthe says to erth : 'This is alle owris'.
But quan erth vpon erth has byggyd his bowris,
Than xal erth for the erth haue scharpe schowris. 8

3 Erthe vpon erth wolde be a kyng,
But hove[2] erth xal to erth thynkyth he no thyng.

4 And of the same erthe mad God man,
And sethe he made that erth & callyd it Adam, 12
For loue of erthe, the wych was woman,
That erth in this erthe fyrst be-gan.

5 Erthe goos on erth & tyllys with hys plowe,
Erthe a-geyn erth holdys it full toght[3], 16
Erthe vpon [erth] stelis hym a slogh[4],
Erthe on this erth thynkys he has neuer i-nowe[5].

6 Erth vpon erthe gos in the weye,
Prykys and prankys on a palfreye; 20
When erth has gotyn erth alle that he maye,
He schal haue but seven fote at his last daye.

7 Than xal not be lykyng vn-to hym
Bu[t][6] an olde sely cloth to wynde erthe in, 24
When erthe is in erth for wormys wyn,
The rof of his hows xal ly on his chyn.

---

[1] or towres, owres, &c. [2] MS. hove for howe. [3] ? error for togh.
[4] Heuser flogh, but MS appears to be slogh as in l. 40. [5] MS. was neuer
non crossed out, has neuer I nowe written above. [6] MS. bu, the last letter
of the word has been erased.

ERTHE UPON ERTHE—THE CAMBRIDGE TEXT. 33

8 [1] When erthe says to erth: 'My rent þou me bryng', [fol. 67, v⁰.]
   Then has erth fro erthe a dolfull partyng.   28

9 How erthe louys erth wondyr me thynke,
   How erth for erth wyll swete and swynke.
   When erth is in erthe broght with-in the brynke,
   What as herth than of erthe but a fowle stynke?   32

10 Erthe wrotys in erth as molys don in molde,
   Erthe vp-on erth glydys as golde,
   As erthe leve in erthe euer more schulde.

11 Erthe vp-on erth mynd euer more þou make   36
   How erthe xal to erth when deth wyll hym take.

12 Be ware, erth, for erthe, for sake of thi sowle,
   Erthe may of erth at þe last take a fowle,
   When erth is in erthe here so long in his slogh.   40

13 Ffor erth gos in erth walkand in vede,
   And erthe rydys on erth on a fayr stede,
   When he was [2] gotyn in erth erth to his mede,
   Than is erth layde in erthe wormys to fede.   44
   Whylke ar the wormys the flesch brede?
   God wote the wormys for to ryght rede.

14 Erthe a-geyn erthe I holde it on-kynde,
   Erthe is as sone wroth as is the wynde,   48
   Swyche fowle erth mekyl may we fynde,
   That wyl speke fayre before vs & falsly be-hynde.

15 When erth vp-on erth be-gynnys to be wroth, [fol. 68, r⁰.]
   Erth vpon erth swerys many a gret othe,   52
   Erth berys pride in herte & in cloth,
   When erth is layde in erth þan xal it be loth.

16 Erthly coveytous makyth erth to be schent,
   Erth for this erth yeldis a gret rent,   56

---

[1] *These two lines form the missing half of v. 3, and are perhaps inserted here with the idea of forming a six-lined stanza.*   [2] *better* has.

If erth in thys erth levyd in good entent
Than dare erthe nevyr recke where that he went.

17 Erth vp-on erth is stronge as a mast,
And erth wyth is erth fyghtys ful fast, 60
There is non so stowte that in erth may hym cast,
And alle xal we be erth at the last.

18 Erthe bygyth hallys & erth bygith towres,
When erth is layd in erth, blayke is his bours; 64
If erth haue welth, he dwellyth in flowres[1],
And if erth haue mys don, he getyth scharpe shours.

19 If erth wyste in erth quat that erth is,
Ther wolde neuer erth in erth do a-mys. 68
God mad erth of erth, & namyd it for his,
Adam of erth in erthly paradys.

20 God walkyd in erth as longe as he wolde,
He had not in this erth but honger & colde, 72
And in this erth also his body was solde,
Here in this erth, whan þat he was xxx^{ti} ȝere olde.

21 God lytyd in erth, blyssed be that stounde! [fol. 68, v°.]
He sauyd hijs herth with many a scharpe wounde, 76
Ffor to sawe erth owght of hell grounde,
He deyd in erth vpon þe rode with many a blody vounde[2].

22 And God ros ovght of the est[3] this erth for to spede,
And went into hell as was gret nede, 80
And toke erth from sorowe þus[4] erth for to spede,
The ryght wey to heuen blys Iesus Cryst vs lede!
fine.

(*The rest of the page is occupied by a coloured picture of a knight and a skeleton with Latin mottoes, v. Introduction, p. xiv.*)

[1] *or* flowris.   [2] wounde.   [3] *MS. clearly* est, *perh. error for* erth.
[4] *MS.* y⁹ = þus, *perh. for* þis.

NOTES.

Page 1. **MS. Harl. 2253.** These four lines were apparently regarded by Wanley, together with the preceding French strophe, as forming part of the poem on the Death of Simon de Montfort, and are not noted by him in the British Museum Catalogue. Böddeker also omitted them from his *Altenglische Dichtungen des MS. Harl. 2253* (Berlin 1878). They were, however, already noted by Pinkerton in 1786, see *Ancient Scottish Poems never before in print . . . from the MS. Collections of Sir Richard Maitland*, ii, Note on p. 466: 'In the same (i. e. Harleian) library, No. 2253, is another of the same kind, beginning,

> Erthe toc of erthe erthe wyth wote.

It is only one stanza; and another piece of one stanza preceding it, both are put by Mr. Wanley, in the Catalogue, as part of a French song on Sir Simon de Montfort, which they follow: but such mistakes frequently arise from the crowded manner of old MSS.' The facsimile opposite the title-page shows the lines as they occur in the MS.

Page 5. **William Billyng's MS.** The 'finely written and illuminated parchment roll' described by William Bateman in his preface to Billyng's *Five Wounds of Christ*, of which forty copies were privately printed by him at Manchester in 1814, contained the following poems:—
1. The Five Wounds of Christ (fifteen stanzas in rime royal).
2. At hygh none whan the belle dothe tylle (eighteen lines).
3. Erth owte of Erth (six stanzas).
4. Pes maketh plente (five lines).

The whole is signed **Willm̄ Billyng**. It has been frequently suggested that Billyng was the author of these poems, but it is evident that he was not the author of *Erthe upon Erthe*, though his may be one of the earliest transcripts of the B version, and the lines *Pes maketh plente* also occur elsewhere, cf. MS. Digby 230 (fifteenth century). He may have been the author of *The Five Wounds of Christ*, but it is more probable, considering the usual origin of other fifteenth-century collections of the kind, that he was merely the collector and transcriber of the texts. Cf. F. J. Furnivall, *Notes and Queries*, IV. iii. 103. It is possible that this may be the William Billyng who, in 1474, became rector of Toft Monks in Norfolk on the presentation of the Provost and Scholars of King's College, Cambridge, and who appears to have held the benefice until 1506 (see *Notes and Queries*, III. iv. 173; Blomefield, *Norfolk*, viii. 63).[1] The parchment roll was formerly preserved in Bateman's collection of antiquities at Lomberdale House, Derbyshire. This collection was broken up and sold after Bateman's death, the archaeological remains being purchased by the Sheffield Museum, and the books and MSS. sold at Messrs. Sotheby, Wilkinson, and Hodge's rooms in 1893, but all attempts to trace Billyng's MS. after the breaking up of the collection have been unsuccessful. A copy of the printed text is in the British Museum.

---

[1] But this is not in agreement with Bateman's opinion as to the age of the original parchment roll (1400-1430), see Introduction, p. xi.

Montgomery's reprint of the poem in 1827 was taken from Bateman's version, and differs from it only in some very slight corrections in spelling. It has been suggested that this reprint was the source of the *Earth upon Earth* Epitaphs which occur, but these were current from the sixteenth century on, and, as has been already pointed out (see Introduction, pp. xxxvi ff.), the usual form of the Epitaph, even in the latest versions, differed from that of the actual poem.

Page 7. MS. Selden Supra 53. This text omits verse 5, and inverts the normal order of verses 4 and 6 (see Table on p. xvii of Introduction). The text is written in a neat hand in the left-hand column on the back of a spare leaf (fol. 159) at the end of the MS., after Lydgate's *Dance of Macabre*. The right-hand column contains Latin scribblings, perhaps by the scribe who re-wrote small portions of *Erthe upon Erthe* (see p. 7, footnotes). A few lines are scribbled in another hand upon the front side of the leaf, which is otherwise blank. The back of the leaf was evidently unprotected, and is much rubbed and worn. The space below Lydgate's last verse and colophon on fol. 158 v⁰ contains two odd stanzas in English in the same metre as Lydgate's poem, beginning 'Let se your hand my ladi, dam emperys', in a hand of the late fifteenth century, and a French stanza of four lines ('Qui met son cuer tout en Deu, Il a son cuer et si a Deu', &c.) in a French hand, perhaps as late as 1500. Both of these were quite possibly inserted in the MS. later than *Erthe upon Erthe*, the exact date of which is indeterminate, but it was probably copied in between 1450 and 1500.

Page 8. MS. Egerton 1995. This MS. was evidently a Commonplace book. Its contents are described by Gairdner, *Collections of a London Citizen* (Camden Society, 1876). The MS. is written throughout in fifteenth-century hand, and appears to be the work of one scribe. Gairdner thinks the whole collection may be ascribed to William Gregory of the Skinners' Company, who was Mayor of London in 1451, and who seems to have been the author of part, at least, of the Chronicle of London at the end of the MS.

Page 10. MS. Brighton. Fiedler's account of this MS. is as follows:—
' Noch eine andre Fassung des Gedichtes habe ich mir vor einigen Jahren aus einer Handschrift abgeschrieben, die damals im Besitze eines Antiquars in Brighton war, über deren weiteren Verbleib ich aber nichts ermitteln könnte. Es war eine Pergamenthandschrift, folio, von 90 Blättern. Sie enthielt eine lateinische Abhandlung über die sieben Sacramente "Oculi Sacerdotis", und auf der ursprünglich frei gebliebenen Rückseite des letzten Blattes war von einer Hand des fünfzehnten Jahrhunderts das englische Gedicht eingetragen.' (*Mod. Lang. Review*, III. iii. 219.)

Page 11. Stratford-on-Avon Inscription. A full account of this inscription has been given in the Introduction, p. xii. The lines ' Whosoo hym be thowghte', there mentioned as being inscribed beneath *Erthe upon Erthe*, are given by Fisher as follows:—

  Whosoo hym be thowght Inwardly and ofte
   How hard hyt ys to flett
  From bede to peyt From peyt to peyne that neuer
   Schall seys Certen
  He wold not doo no syn all ļis world to wynne.

The same lines are found on other monumental inscriptions. Weever (*Ancient Funeral Monuments*, p. 425) mentions them as occurring in sixteenth-century inscriptions in Churches at Saffron Walden and Faversham respectively, and Rogers (*Monuments and Monumental Inscriptions in Scotland*, ii. 210) quotes them from a tombstone in the parish of Dun. The following version is from Bodl. MS. Tanner 407, fol. 36, v° (sixteenth century):—

> He that hath thoughte
> ful in-wardly and ofte
> how hard it is to flyt
> fro bedde on to pyt
> fro pytte on to pyne
> whiche neuyr schal haue fyne
> for alle thys world to wynne
> wold not do a synne.

Page 16. MS. Laud Misc. 23. This is the only text which is not written in metrical lines. The MS. being small, it was not as a rule possible to fit one line of the poem into a single line of the page, and the run-on lines involved waste of space. The scribe wrote verse 1 in metrical lines, verses 2 and 3 as if in two long lines, and the remainder of the poem in paragraphs, each paragraph coinciding with a verse. Each new line or paragraph is indicated by a red capital, and the metrical lines are distinguished by pause-marks (✓, ·, ✓, |), and by touching up the first letter of the line in red. In vv. 6, 7, and 8, the scribe appears to have lost count of the lines, as the three verses are written in two paragraphs, and letters in the middle of a line are often marked in red. At the top of the first leaf a later hand has scribbled the words *haue made me*. A few other such scribbles occur elsewhere in the MS.

l. 26 (p. 17). *Thi body that was rank and louyd of alle men, is hatyd.* The reading is inferior to MS. Lambeth, l. 27:

> þan þi bodi þat was rank & undeuout of alle men is bihatid—

and the change led to the placing of the pause (indicated in the MS.) after *men*.

l. 27. *Out of the erthe cam to this erthe his wantyng garnement.* This line seems to be a compromise between the readings of MSS. Lamb. and Rawl. P.
(*MS. Lamb. 28*)

> Out of þis erþe cam to þis erþe þis wrecchid garnement.

(*MS. Rawl. P. 37*)

> Oute of the erthe cam the erthe wantynge his garnament.

But the rest of the verse follows Lamb. rather than Rawl. P., cf. *ruly, raggid and rent, hidous turment*, beside Rawl. P. *disgesily ragged and to-rent, ful grete turment*.

l. 34 has the correct reading *stinke*, as in MSS. Harl. 4486 and Rawl. P.; Lamb. repeats *swynk*.

l. 39 (p. 18). *Wolde therfore this erthe on this erthe on this hertly thinke*, is superior to the exaggeratedly long line in Lamb. 40, but both are inferior to MS. Rawl. P., ll. 53, 54, where the correct rime is preserved:

> thinkynge : risynge : rekenynge : kynge.

NOTES.

l. 47. *Lord God that erthe madist & for the erthe suffredist peynys ille.* It is difficult to determine what was the original form of this line. The readings of the other texts which have the verse are as follows :—

(*Harl. 4486, 33*)

Now Lorde that madyst for erthe & sufferdyst paynes ille.

(*Lamb. 48*)

O þou Lord that madist þis erþe for þis erþe & suffridist heere peynes ille.

(*Rawl. P. 125–6*).

Lord God that erthe tokist in erthe And suffredist paynes ful stille.

Possibly MS. Laud has transposed the *and*, and the correct reading should be *that erthe madist for the erthe & suffredist paynes ille*, in which case Harl. 4486 has merely omitted the first *erthe*, while the other two texts have modified the older version.

Page 24. MS. Porkington 10. *Erthe upon Erthe* is preceded by the two following stanzas :—

    Lo wordly folkes thou3 þis processe of dethe
    Be not swete, ne synke not in your mynde.
    When age commyþ & schorteth is her brethe,
    And dethe commyþ, he is not far behynde ;
    Then her dyscression schal wel knov & fynde
    That to have mynd of deþ it is ful nesseserry,
    Ffor deth wyl come ; dovtles he wyl not long tarry.

    Of what estate 3e be, 3ovng or wold,
    That redyth vppon þis dredful storrye,
    As in a myrrovr her 3e may be-holde
    The ferful ende of al your joy & glorie ;
    Therfor þis mater redvs vs to yovr memory :—
    3e þat syttyþ nowe hye vppon þe whele,
    Thynke vppon yovr end, & alle schal be we[le].

The MS. is in Lord Harlech's library at Brogyntyn (formerly Porkington) near Oswestry, Salop.

Page 28. MS. Balliol 354. l. 48. *Go to seynt Poulis, & see þer the portratowre.* Cf. Stow, *Survey of London*, 1598: 'There was also one great cloister on the north side of this church (St. Paul's), environing a plot of ground, of old time called Pardon churchyard ... About this cloister was artificially and richly painted the Dance of Machabray, or Dance of Death, commonly called the Dance of Paul's ; the like whereof was painted about St. Innocent's cloister at Paris, in France. The metres or poesy of this dance were translated out of French into English by John Lidgate, monk of Bury, and with the picture of death leading all estates, painted about the cloister, at the special request and in the dispence of Jenken Carpenter, in the reign of Henry V.'

Ibid. 'John Carpenter, townclerk of London, in the reign of Henry V, caused with great expense to be curiously painted upon board, about the north cloister of Paule's, a monument of Death leading all estates, with the speeches of Death, and answer of every state. This cloister was pulled down 1549.'

Cf. Sir T. More, *Works* (ed. 1557, folio), p. 77 : 'We wer never so gretly moved by the beholding of the Daunce of Deth pictured in Paule's.'

Page 30. Maitland MS. Omitted by Pinkerton from his printed text of the Maitland MS. as 'a silly jingling piece, shewing the vanity of man, who is but earth, building upon earth : priding himself in gold which is but earth', &c. Pinkerton also knew of 'several pieces of the same kind in MSS. of Old English poetry', see Note on MS. Harl. 2253, p. 36. He had strong views against the indiscriminate printing of old MSS., and was unwilling to sacrifice 'the character of a man of taste to that of an antiquary; as of all characters he should the least chuse that of an hoarder of ancient dirt'.

Page 32. MS. Cambridge (Univ. Libr. I. 1. iv. 9). l. 17. The reading *slogh* is supported by Professor Skeat. It is difficult to see what meaning could be attached to *flogh*, as in Heuser's text.

Page 33. l. 48. *As wroth as the wynde* was a favourite mediaeval proverb. Cf. *Sir Gawayne and the Grene Knight*, l. 319 : he wex as wroth as wynde; *Piers Plowman*, C. iv. 486 : As wroth as the wynd wex Mede ther-after; *Richard the Redeles*, iii. 153 : thei woll be wroth as the wynde.

ANALOGUES.

It may be of interest to note here some other instances of the use of the theme *Earth upon Earth*, not immediately connected with the poem under discussion.

An early instance of the phrase occurs in a Poem on the Death of Edward IV, written by Skelton probably soon after the event (9th April, 1483), beginning *Miseremini mei ye that ben my ffryndys*. Verse 2 runs as follows :—

> I slepe now in molde, as it is naturall
> That erth vnto erth hath his reuerture :
> What ordeyned God to be terestyall,
> Without recours to the erth of nature?
> Who to lyue euer may himselfe assure?
> What is it to trust on mutabilyte,
> Sith that in this world nothing may indure?
> For now am I gone, that late was in prosperyte :
> To presume thervppon, it is but a vanyte,
> Not certayne, but as a chery fayre full of wo :
> Reygned not I of late in greate felycite?
> *Et, ecce, nunc in pulvere dormio!*
> (*Poetical Works of Skelton*, ed. Dyce, I. i; London, 1843).

The poem was inserted amongst the unprinted works of Lydgate, who could not have been alive in 1483, cf. MS. Harl. 4011, fol. 169, v°, where it occurs among Lydgate's works.

In John Taylor's *Travels of Twelve-Pence*, 1630 folio (Spenser Soc. reprint, p. 82), this verse occurs :—

> Far[1] though from *Earth* man hath originall,
> And to the *Earth*, from whence he came doth fall,
> Though he be Earth, & can claime nought but earth,
> (As the fraile portion due vnto his birth)
> Yet many thousands that the earth doth breed,
> Haue no place (certain) where to lodge or feed.

[1] ? for.

The following lines occur in a small volume called *The Compleat Bell-Man, being a Pattern for all sorts of People to take notice of the most remarkable Times and Dayes in the Year,* by H. Crouch (seventeenth century). The book contains thirty-nine verses, for Saint-Days and Anniversaries chiefly, a few being on more general subjects. The last verse, No. 39, *Upon the day of Doom,* runs as follows:—

>When Earth of Earth shall turn to Earth
>That was but Earth even from its Birth,
>Then Earth from Earth shall rise again
>To endlesse joy, or endlesse pain,
>Let Earth then serve and please his Maker
>That Earth of Heaven may be pertaker.

The following is an Epitaph on Roger Earth of Dinton, Wilts, died 1634 (see E. R. Suffling, *Epitaphia,* p. 81):—

>From Earth wee came, to Earth wee must returne,
>Witness this EARTH that Lyes within this VRNE.
>Begott by EARTH: Borne also of Earth's WOMBE,
>74 yeares lived EARTH, now Earth's his TOMBE.
>In Earth EARTH'S Body Lyes Vnder this STONE,
>But from this Earth to Heauen EARTH'S soule is gone.

Another later epitaph is quoted by Suffling, p. 339, from Loughter, Glamorganshire, without name or date:—

>O Earth! O Earth observe this well,
> That Earth to Earth must go to dwell,
>That Earth to Earth must close remain
> Till Earth for Earth shall come again.

APPENDIX I.

THE three following *Erthe* poems, in Latin, French, and English respectively, were discovered too late for inclusion in the text. They represent renderings of the same poem in the three languages, and are preserved on the back of a Roll[1] in the Public Record Office, containing a copy of the Ordinances of the fifth year of Edward II (of which other copies exist in the British Museum, the Record Office, and the Treasury at Canterbury). The poems in question are written on the back of the Roll, towards the end, the Latin and French in parallel columns, and the English below, five verses under the Latin, and four under the French. They are preceded by a number of Latin recipes in another hand, and a few in French follow. The handwriting of the poems is smaller and neater than that of the Ordinances, or the Latin recipes, but was ascribed by Hunter[2] to the time of Edward II, and may perhaps be assigned to the fourteenth century. The French is fourteenth-century Anglo-French, and the texts probably belong to that century, though this copy of them may not have been made until after 1400.

A nineteenth-century transcript of the poems exists in the British Museum, Addit. MS. 25478 (fol. 1-3), described in the Catalogue as containing 'Transcripts of miscellaneous English poetry, with a few Latin pieces, chiefly derived from MS. sources: xivth to xixth century'. The binding is marked 'Collectanea Hunteriana', and the MS. was acquired with various others of the Hunter collection in 1863. The handwriting varies, and these three poems are not in Hunter's own hand. The transcript is headed 'Copy of a Poem in Latin, French, and English, which is written in a hand of the reign of Edward II, on the dorse of a Roll which contains a copy of the ordinances of the fifth year of Edward II, which are printed in the Statutes of the Realm I. 157-168'. The text given below has been collated with this transcript, and variant readings in the latter given in the footnotes under the name Hunter (H.).

The British Museum transcript was discovered by Miss Helen Sandison of Bryn Mawr, U.S.A., who kindly acquainted me with her discovery, and was of great assistance in the search for the original Roll, which was eventually found in a bundle awaiting rearrangement at the Record Office. A large stain on the original text has rendered a considerable portion of the Latin and a few words in the French almost illegible, and Hunter's transcript has left blanks at these points. Mr. S. C. Ratcliff, of the Record Office, has given me much kind and courteous assistance in deciphering the missing words, thanks to which I have been able to fill up all the gaps, except that in verse 8, l. 3 of the Latin. Hunter's text at this point runs as follows:—

    4. l. 4. Sic t'ra put^{e}dinis . . . t're venas.
    6. l. 4. Terra t'rā faciat flere ieu . . . . .
    7.   De t'ra resurg'e t'ra deb . . . .
       Et quod t'ra meruit . . . .
       Hic dum terra vix'it . . . .
       Ut in t'ra valeat . . . . . dere
    8.   Adu'sus t'rigenas . . . . terra stabit
       Et t'rā int'roga . . . . abit
       Terra finem cap . . . . gabit
       Quod terra promiserat t'ra . . . urgabit.

and in the French:—
    9. l. 2. Sayt cydaunt a la tere qe tere soit sauve
       . . . . eyne de tere ou tere est benure.

---

[1] Ex^r. K. R. Parl. Proceedings, Bdle. 1 (Old No. $\frac{645}{21}$).
[2] Joseph Hunter, the antiquary (1783-1861), Sub-Commissioner of the Public Records 1833, Assistant-Keeper of the Records 1838.

APPENDIX I.

RECORD OFFICE ROLL (Ex^r. K. R. Parl. Proc., Bdle. 1).
LATIN TEXT (in left column).

1 In terra cum terra sit fraude perquisita, [MS. Addit. 25478,
  Terra terre vermibus sic putressit trita,   fol. 2, r°]
  Terra terram deseret, erit et finita,
  Terra tunc a terren[i]s[1] mox erit oblita.   4

2 Terra per superbiam terram cum ascendit,
  Terra tunc cupidine terram comprehendit,
  Terra morti proximans terram dat et vendit,
  Ad terram viuencium terra manus tendit.   8

3 Terra terram speculans non iustificari,
  Et ad terre terminum terram inclinari.
  Terra terre seruiens vult[2] refrigerari,
  Et terra terribilis in terra locari.   12

4 In terra quid possidet terra nisi penas
  Quando terra respicit terram lite plenas,
  Et terram deficere tanquam terre tenas,
  Sic terra putredinis intrat[3] terre venas?   16

5 Terra non considerat terram firma mente,
  Atque terra labitur in terram repente,
  Terram suo sanguine terra redimente,
  Terram potens eruit de terra dolente.   20

ENGLISH TEXT (in left column, below Latin)

1 Whanne eorthe hath eorthe wiþ wrong igete, [MS. Addit. 25478,
  And eorthe in eorthe biginneþ to alete,   fol. 3, r°]
  And eorthe in eorthe wiþ wormes is afrete,
  Thanne eorthe is on eorthe sone forȝete.   4

2 Wanne eorthe ouer eorthe þorw prude styeþ,
  And eorthe toward eorthe þorw coueytise wryeþ,
  & eorthe into eorthe toward þe deþ hyeþ,
  Þanne eorthe aȝeyn eorthe toward heuene crieþ.[4]   8

3 Whan eorthe juynt eorthe so luþer[5] to aweklen,
  & eorthe on þat eorthe allewey[6] bi helden,

---

[1] *MS.* aterrens *as one word.*   [2] *MS.* wlt.   [3] *this word is very obscure, and is omitted by Hunter; portions of* nt *and the second* t *can be seen.*
[4] *H.* b^{l}eþ.   [5] *H.* luþ.   [6] *the MS. has a gap after* allewey *with space for a word of five or six letters, but there is no erasure nor trace of any omission.*

APPENDIX I. 43

FRENCH TEXT (in right column).

1 Qu*a*nt te*r*re auera en¹ terre large terre gayne, [MS. Addit. 25478,
   & te*r*re serra en terre a la mort liuere,   fol. 1, r°]
   Puis ert tere en tere de v*er*myne mange,
   Dounc vendra tere en tere & toust ert oblie.   4

2 Qu*a*nt tere sour te*rr*e de orgoyl descline,
   & tere ils² [vers] tere par coueitise encline,
   Dounc tere ils² [vers] tere se treit a Ruyne,
   & tere a haute tere requeit medicine.   8

3 Qu*a*nt tere ne peot de te*r*re la malueste sourueyndre,
   Par force deit tere de te*r*re temptaciouns esteyndre,
   Encontre la fiele tere sa tere deit refreyndre,
   Qu*a*nt tere leue en tere face sa tere moyndre.   12

4 Quey ad tere de tere forq*ue* dolour & peygne
   Qu*a*nt tere veyt en terre soun enemi demeygne,
   & tere coust en tere a la mort certeyne³,
   & tere pase en tere par frelete humeyne?   16

5 O tu cheytiue tere de tere, remembrez   [MS. Addit. 25478,
   Vo*us* estes pris de tere & tere deuendrez,   fol. 1, v°]
   Pensez coment en tere & par tere pecchez,
   & tere fiust en tere tant fortment⁵ rechatez.   20

ENGLISH TEXT (in left column, below Latin).

   & eorthe on eorthe sone bigynneþ for to elden,
   Hou may þat⁶ eorthe on eorthe wo⁶ belden?   12

4 What haueþ eorthe on eorthe bote þouȝt⁷ and⁷ wo,
   Whan eorthe iseoþ⁸ eorthe his dedliche fo,
   & eorthe into eorthe so sone gynneþ guo,
   & eorthe iworthe to eorthe alle we sullen so?   16

5 Alas why naþ eorthe⁹ in eorthe is þouȝt,
   Hou eorthe is on eorthe wiþ synnes of-souȝt,
   & eorthe was in eorthe so mychfulliche ibouȝt,
   Þat eorthe þorw eorthe ne foelle¹⁰ to nouȝt?   20

---

¹ *inserted above the line.* ² *MS. has* ils, *surely a scribal error; the original had probably* uers = vers '*towards*', *with the MS. compendium for* er, *written over and confused with the second stroke of the* u *so as to look like* il. ³ *H.* e'teyne. ⁴ *H.* peisez. ⁵ *H.* foilment. ⁶,⁷ *in fresher ink above the line.* ⁸ *MS.* iꞅoeþ. ⁹ *above the line.* ¹⁰ *MS.* foelle; ? falle.

APPENDIX I.

6 Terra quando respicit terram terminare,
Terra terram debuit sese castigare,
Terra terram valeat vt humiliare,
Terra terram faciat flere ieiunare[1]. 24

7 De terra resurgere terra debet vere[1],
Et quod terra meruit terra[1] possidere[1],
Hic dum terra vixerit terra[1] valet[1] flere[1],
Ut in terra valeat terra[1] post[1] gaudere[1]. 28

8 Aduersus terrigenas quando[1] terra stabit, [MS. Addit. 25478,
Et terram interrogans terra[1] tunc[1] culpabit[1], fol. 2, v°]
Terra finem cap[ia]t terram[1] ... gabit[2],
Quod terra promiserat terra tunc[1] negabit[3]. 32

9 In terra qui mortuus & in terra natus
Ffuit[4], terram protegat sic & terre[5] gratus,
Vt in terra quilibet de terra formatus,
Terre ponat terminum terre comendatus. 36

10 In terra cum Angeli terram suscitabunt,
In terra terribiles tube resonabunt,
De terra terrigene corpora leuabunt,
Et ad terre judicem terre tunc clamabunt. 40

11 O tu terre domine! terre miserere,
Et terra respiciens terenos tuere,
In terra deficimus, terra sumus vere,
Nos in terra glorie terram fac videre. 44

(in right column, below French)

6 Whan eorthe iseoþ eorthe to endinge drawe,
& eorthe on eorthe wiþ deþ is islawe,
& eorthe on eorthe wiþ wormes in ignawe,
Þanne eorthe may eorthe him seluen iknawe. 24

7 Wan eorthe ssal of eorthe netfulliche aryse, [MS. Addit. 25478
& eorthe on eorthe ihere þilke assise fol. 3, v°]
Þer eorthe ne may eorthe noþer[6] lere ne wise,
Þanne eorthe sal on eorthe grimliche agrise. 28

---

[1] *All words marked* [1] *are omitted in H.'s transcript, the MS. at this point being stained and obscure.* [2] *Professor Robinson Ellis suggests* obiurgabit *here, which would fit the space: there is room for 2-3 letters, and possibly a trace of an* r *contraction.* [3] H. urgabit. [4] *obscure,* H. fuit; MS. *might be* ffinit. [5] H. t'roe. [6] H. neþer.

6 Quant tere veyt que tere se treit a la mort,
& tere nad en tere forque poure confort,
Quant tere moert[1] en tere ni ad nul resort,
Merueille est que tere de tere nad retort. 24

7 Quant tere[2] deit de tere leuer sodeynement,
Tere vendra en tere pur oyer jugement,
Dounc auera tere en tere dolour & turment,
Si tere neit fet en tere bon amendement. 28

8 Angeles vendrount en tere la tere resusciter,
& dirrount a la tere de tere couent leuer,
Deuant le Roy de tere en tere deuez aller[3],
Que[4] soffri en tere pur tere dolour amer. 32

9 Jesu, que pur la tere en tere fiust ne,
Soyt eydaunt[5] a la tere que tere soit sauue,
& nos meyne[6] de tere ou tere est benure,
Kar si sumes en tere par tere turmente[7]. 36

10 Dolour est en tere par tere & par mer,
Ffaus est tere en tere & tere desir auer,
Pluis ne voil en tere ore[8] de tere chaunter.
Dieu deynt tere en tere de viuauns habiter. Amen. 40

(in right column, below French)

8 Þanne eorthe sal to eorthe holden gret cheste,
& eorthe asken eorthe were is hiere byheste
Þat eorthe byhet eorthe allewey to leste,
Wanne eorthe turneþ to eorthe toward Helle feste. 32

9 Houre Louerd þat on eorthe for eorthe was iboren,
On eorthe of eorthe wiþ wounden to-toren,
Wyte eorthe from eorthe þat ne be furloren,
& bringe eorthe to þat eorthe þer beþ his icoren. 36
          Amen.

[1] *H*. mo ert. [2] *inserted in margin; H. omits.* [3] *H*. aler. [4] *H*. le.
[5] *H*. sayt eydaunt. [6] *H*. . . . . . . eyne. [7] *H*. t'menti. [8] *H*. ou.

APPENDIX I.

It will be seen that the Latin and French versions do not correspond exactly with the English text, the French in particular being a mere paraphrase of it, but this was, no doubt, largely due to the exigencies of the rime. The French text has ten stanzas as against nine in the English poem, and the Latin has eleven, the additional stanzas being an expansion of the theme after the manner of Anglo-Latin poems of the kind. It is evident both from the variant attempts at expansion of the text in the Latin and French, and from the greater freshness and more skilful use of the play on the word *erthe* of the English text, that the latter is the original, and this supports the view already expressed (Introd. p. xxxiii) as to the relation of the English and Latin versions in MS. Harl. 913. It is improbable, at least, that the *Erthe upon Erthe* poems should all be derived from two Latin poems, the differences between which are too great to admit of a common original, but which were both translated into English verse, and became, in course of time, modified and popularized. On the other hand, the fact that one fourteenth-century poem of the kind had been supplied with a Latin rendering might easily account for an attempt at Latin and French translations in the case of a second, and there seems to be reason for believing that the author of the latter text was acquainted with the poem in MS. Harl. 913. As has been already noted in the Introduction (p. xxxii), the first line of the English version corresponds in idea with that of the text in MS. Harl. 913:

Whan erþ haþ erþ iwanne wiþ wow.

and in actual wording with that of the *Song on the Times*:

When erthe hath erthe i-gette.

Otherwise no verbal connexion can be traced with any of the texts of *Erthe upon Erthe*, though the phrase *eorthe on eorthe* recurs four times, and there is, of necessity, some similarity of treatment and idea. Thus the remainder of verse 1 contains a reference to the destruction by worms, mentioned in MS. Harl. 913, v. 2, and in the Cambridge text, vv. 7 and 13, as well as to the proverb that the dead are soon forgotten, cf. MS. Harl. 913, v. 4 (Introd. p. xxxi); verse 5 exhorts man to think of death, as does v. 6 of the B Version; and the poem ends with a prayer, as do MSS. Harl. 4486, Lambeth, Laud, Titus, and Rawl. P., as well as Rawl. C., and the Cambridge text. But the wording, and, in the two latter cases, the treatment, is different, and the general similarity is less than might be expected from the triteness of the theme. Both the A and the B Version lay stress on the contrast between man's present earthly glory and his future mingling with the dust, whereas the text in the Appendix dwells on the inevitableness of death, the pains of death, and the future judgement (only mentioned here and in MS. Harl. 913). The poem appears to represent an individual treatment of the subject, suggested perhaps by the text in MS. Harl. 913 with its Latin rendering, and possibly also influenced by the *Song on the Times* in the same MS. It may be regarded as being ultimately based, like MS. Harl. 913, on the short stanzas current at the beginning of the fourteenth century, and as furnishing additional evidence of the early popularity of the theme, a popularity which gave rise at first to individual poems like this and MS. Harl. 913, and later to the repetition and expansion of one common type as in the B Version. But, unlike MS. Harl. 913, this text stands apart from the more popular types of the poem, and has no connexion with either the B Version or the Cambridge text. It must therefore have been written before the short normal type of the B Version became current, and probably before it took shape as a poem of several stanzas, that is before 1400. The want of close connexion between it and the more usual types of the poem given above, makes the omission of it from the text the less to be regretted, since it represents a side-issue rather than a link in the development of the poem as here treated.

APPENDIX II.

B Version 19.
MS. Trinity College Cambridge R. 3. 21. [fol. 33, v⁰.]

(This text represents the normal seven-stanza type of the B version, but without precise verbal agreement with any text printed above.)

1   E   rthe vppon erthe so wondyrly wrought,
Erthe opon erthe hath gete a dignite of nought,
Erthe opon erthe hath set all hys thought
How erthe opon erthe may on hyght be brought.   4

2 Erthe opon erthe wold be a kyng;
But how that erthe goth to erthe thynketh he nothyng.
When erthe byddyth erthe hys rent home bryng,
Than erthe from erthe hath full hard partyng.   8

3 Erthe opon erthe wynneth castelles and towres;
Than seyth erthe to erthe: 'Thys ys all owres'.
When erthe opon erthe hath bylde halles and bowres,
Then shall erthe fro erthe suffre sharpe showres.   12

4 Erthe goth opon erthe as molde opon molde,
Erthe goth opon erthe and glytereth as golde,
Lyke as erthe to erthe neue*r* go sholde.
And yet shall erthe to erthe rather then he wolde.   16

5 Why erthe loueth erthe wondyr I may thynke,
Or why erthe for erthe wyll other swete or s[w]ynke,
Ffor when erthe in-to erthe ys brought wi*th*yn the brynke,
Than shall erthe of erthe haue a foule stynke.   20

6 Lo erthe opon erthe considere well thow may
How erthe co*m*meth to erthe nakyd alway.
Why shuld erthe than opon erthe go stout and gay
Seth erthe in-to erthe shall passe in a pore aray?   24

7 I counsell erthe opon erthe that wykkyd hath wrought,
Whyle erthe ys opon erthe to torne vp hys thought,
And pray God opon erthe that all erthe hath wrought,
That erthe out of erthe to blysse may be brought. Amen.   28

                Memorare nouissima.

APPENDIX II.

B Version 20.

MS. Trinity College Cambridge B. 15. 39. [fol. 170.]

This text (in MS. not written in metrical lines) preserves 9 stanzas of the 12-stanza version in MSS. Lambeth and Laud, and appears to represent a distinct and perhaps older copy of the original of these two. The mistake in v. 8 precludes its being the original.

De terra plasmasti me, *etc.*

1 [1] Erþe out of erþe is wondirli wrouȝt,
   Erþe of erþe haþ gete a dignite of nouȝt,
   Erþe vpon erþe haþ sett al his þouȝt,
   Howe þat erþe vpon erþe may be hiȝ brouȝt.   4

2 Erþe vpon erþe wolde ben a king;
   But how erþe schal to erþe þenkiþ he no þing;
   Whanne þan erþe biddiþ erþe hise rentis hoom bring,
   Þanne schal erþe out of erþe haue a piteuous partinge.   8

3 Erþe vpon erþe wynneþ castels and tours,
   Þanne seiþ erþe to erþe : 'þis is all ouris.'
   Whanne erþe vpon [2] erþe [haþ biggid] [3] up his bouris,
   Þan schal erþe for erþe for [4] suffre scharpe schouris.   12

4 Erþe gooþ upon erþe as molde upon moolde,
   So gooþ erþe upon erþe al glitiringe in golde,
   Lijk as erþe vnto erþe neuere go scholde,
   And ȝit schal erþe vnto erþe raþir þan he wolde.   16

5 O þou [fol. 170, v°] wrecchid erþe þat in þe erþe trauellist niȝt
    & day,
   To florische þe erþe, to peinte þe erþe wiþ wantowne aray,
   Ȝit schalt þou erþe for al þi erþe, make þou it neuere so queinte
    or gay,
   Out of þis erþe in-to þe erþe, þere to klinge as a clot of clay.   20

6 O wrecchid man whi art þou proud þat art of erþe makid?
   Hidir brouȝtist þou no schroud, but pore come þou and nakid.
   Whanne þi soule is went out & þi bodi in [5] erþe rakid,
   Þan þi [bodi] [6] þat was rank & bilouid of al men is bihatid.   24

---

[1] *MS. erron. begins with a capital* D.   [2] *Crossed out in MS.*   [3] *Omitted in MS.*   [4] *So in MS.*   [5] *MS. is erron. for* in   [6] *Omitted in MS.*

APPENDIX II.

7 Out of þis erþe cam to þis erþe þis wantinge grarnement[1];
 To hide þis erþe, to happe þis erþe, to him was cloþing lent;
 But now[2] gooþ erþe upon erþe, ruli raggid & rent,
 Þerfore schal erþe vndir þe erþe haue hidous turment. 28

8 Þerfore þou erþe vpon erþe þat wikkidli hast wrouȝt,
 While þat erþe is upon erþe turne aȝen þi þouȝt,
 & pray to God vpon erthe þat [al þe erþe haþ][3] wrouȝt,
 þat erþe vpon erþe to blis may be brouȝt. 32

9 Now Lord þat erþe madist for erþe & suffridist peines ille,
 Lete neuere þis erþe for þis erþe mischeue ne spille,
 But þat þis erþe in þis erþe be euere worchinge þi wille,
 So that erþe fro þis erþe stie vp to þin hiȝ hille. AMEN. 36

Memento homo quod cinis es. et in cinerem reuerteris.
Ffac bene dum viuis. post mortem viuere si vis.

A man þat wilneþ for to profite in þe wey of perfeccioun & souvereinli to plese God. he muste studie bisili for to haue þese maters in his herte þat folewiþ here aftir.

First biþenke þee [etc.]

---

[1] *erron. for* garnement [2] erþe vpon erþe *inserted after* now *in MS. and crossed out.* [3] *MS. erroneously repeats, from l.* 29, þat vickidli hast wrouȝt.

GLOSSARY.

Abbey, *sb.* 13.6. *perh. erron. for* nobley.
Agaste, *a.* aghast 25.54.
Agayn(e), ageyn, aȝen, ayen, *adv.* again 13.30, 15.45, 21.34, 24.20, 28.54; *prep.* against 33.47.
Aȝenrisynge, *sb.* resurrection 15.41.
Al, all, *a.* 28.49, 53.
Ale, *sb.* 25.60.
Almis, *sb.* alms 24.24.
Also, *adv.* 28.37, 34.73.
Alway(e), all(e) way(e), *adv.* always 7.14, 9.22, 10.22, 25.32, 29.58, &c.
Amende, *vb. imp.* 24.18.
Amys, *adv.* amiss 34.68.
Answerid, *vb.* 3 *p. pr.* answereth 2.25.
Apone, ap(p)one, *prep., var. of* upon 6.3, 5, 9; 7.1, 2, 3; 9.1, 2, &c.
Ar, 3.50. ? *erron. for* a.
Aray(e), array, *sb.* array 7.16, 8.26, 19.18, 21.64, 30.24, &c., &c.
Askeþ, askip, *vb.* 3 *p. pr.* 2.25, 39.
Auyse, *vb. imp.* bethink thyself, consider 22.98.
Awaked, *vb. pr. pl.* awaken 1.6.
Away, *adv.* 30.22, 31.22.
Ay, *adv.* aye 25.58.

Bare, *a.* 22.88.
Be, *vb.* 5.4, 5, 6.4, 5, &c., &c.; *imp.* 3.63, 22.97, 24.23; *subj.* 13.9, 14.35, &c.; 2 *p. pr.* art. 1.5, 15.24, 45, 19.21; 3 *p. pr.* is, ys 2.16, 17, 40, 42, 3.49, 50, 7.1, &c., es 6.1, 10, 19; *pr. pl.* be, beth 2.38, 3.66, 7.10, 28.43, 45, bythe 13.14, byne 25.52, ar 30.10, 31.10, 33.45; 2 *p.p.* were 1.5, 2.29, 22.92; 3 *p.p.* was 15.29, 21.40, 23.101, &c.; *p. pl.* were 27.21, 28.27.
Before, beffore, byfore, *adv.* before 28.44, 52; *prep.* 22.100, 33.50.
Begilynge, *sb.* beguiling 23.106.
Begynnynge, *sb.* beginning 23.102.
Begynnys, *vb.* 3 *p. pr.* begins 33.51; 3 *p. p.* began 28 31, 32.14; *pp.* bigun 2.29.
Beholde, *vb. imp.* behold 12.25.

Behynde, *prep.* behind 33.50.
Beriþ, berriþ, berys, *vb.* 3 *p. pr.* bears 2.15, 28, 33.53.
Beste, *a.* best 12.21.
Bete, *pp.* beaten 23.116.
Betyme, *adv.* betimes 24.18, 25.57.
Be ware, *vb. imp.* beware 22.97, 33.38.
Biddethe, biddis, biddith, bydd-es, -eth,-is,-ys,-yth(e), bydyth, *vb.* 3 *p. pr.* bids 5.7, 7.7, 8.9, 9.7, 10.7, &c.; 3 *p.p.* bade 25.36.
Biddyngis, *sb.* biddings 23.124.
Bigged, biggid, -it, bygged(e), -id, -it, -yd, -yt, *pp.* built, 6.11, 7.11, 10.11, 12.11, 13.15, 14.14, 17.13, 19.11, 30.11, 31.11, 32.7; ON. byggja.
Bihatid, *pp.* hated 15.27.
Bild, *v. imp.* build 3.64; 2 *p. pr.* bildist 22 79; 3 *p. pr.* bilt, 3.65, byldyth 5.13; *pp.* bildyd, billid, bylde, byllyd, 5.11, 8.13, 11.11, 20.22, 27.11.
Bink, bynk, *sb.* bank 30.19, 31.19. L. Scots.
Blak, blayke, *a.* black 3.66, 34.64.
Blesse, *sb., var. of* blis, bliss 29.6.
Blis, blys, blysse, *sb.* bliss 4.77, 7.24, 8.30, 9.28, 10.28, &c.
Blode, *sb.* blood 25.46.
Blynde, *a.* blind 25.37.
Blyssed, *pp.* blessed 34.75.
Bodi, body, *sb.* 15.26, 27, 17.25, 26, 34.73.
Bold, *sb.* dwelling 3.64.
Bold, *a.* 28.42.
Bon, *sb.* bone 22.88.
Borowes, *sb. erron. for* bowres, bowers 10.11.
Both, *pron.* 28.41.
Bour(e)s, bour(r)is, bourys, bowres, -is, -ys, *sb. pl.* bowers 3.66, 5.11, 6.11, 8 13, 9.11, 12.11, 14.14, 17.13, 27.11, &c.
Bouȝte, *pp. erron. for* broȝt 26.70.
Brede, *sb.* bread 25.60.
Bredis, *vb.* 3 *p. pr.* breeds 6.7; (*perh. erron. for* biddis); 3 *p. p.* brede 33.45.

GLOSSARY.

Brente, *pp.* burnt 10.19.
Brether, *sb. pl.* brothers 28.44.
Bring, bryng(e), *vb.* 5.7, 6.7, 7.7 14.10, &c.; *imp.* bryng 33.27; 2 *p. p.* broght, brou3ttist, broutyst 15.25, 17.24, 19.22; *pp.* brocht, bro(u)ght(e), broht, brou3t(e), brouþt, browt(h)e, 5.4, 6.4, 7.4, 8.6, 9.3, 10.4, 28, 13.8, 14.7, 30.4, &c.
Brink(e), brynk(e), *sb.* brink (of the grave) 5.19, 6.19, 15.34, 17.33, 27.19, &c.; *pl.* brynkes 10.19.
Byggis, bygith, -yth, *vb.* 3 *p. pr.* builds *v.* bigged 12.9, 34.63.
Byrthe, *sb.* birth 26.72.

Calle, *sb.* summons 12.23.
Callyd, *vb.* 3 *p. p.* called, named 32.12.
Carayne, caryon, *sb.* carrion 2.39, 24.30.
Care, *sb.* care, anxiety 24.11.
Case, *sb.* 26.64.
Cast, *vb.* 34.61.
Castles, castells, casteles, castels, castells, -es, -is, -ys, castylles, *sb. pl.* castles 3.65, 5.9, 6.9, 7 9, 8.11, 9.9, &c., &c.
Certayn, certeyn, *a.* certain 28.53, 56.
Chyn, chynne, *sb.* chin 2.17, 32.26.
Clay(e), *sb.* 15.23, 17.22, 19.20, 21.68.
Clinge, clynge, klyng, *vb.* to shrink up, decay 15.23, 17.22, 19.20, 21.68. Cf. *E. E. Allit. P. A.* 856, oure corses in clottez clynge, *Hymns to Virgin and Christ*, p. 85, in coold clay now schal y clinge.
Closed, closit, *pp.* enclosed, shut up 28.39, 30.19, 31.19.
Clot, clotte, *sb.* clot of clay, a hardened lump of earth, 15.23, 17.22, 19.20, 21.68; *replaced by* NE. clod.
Cloth, *sb.* 32.24, 33.53.
Cloth, *vb. imp.* clothe 25.36.
Clothing(e), *sb.* 15.29, 17.28, 21.40.
Cold(e), *sb.* 12.15, 28.43, 34.72.
Com, *vb.* come 12.23; 2 *p. pr.* commys 25.32; 3 *p. pr.* comes, comeþ, commeth, comyth(e), commyth 7.14, 8.24, 9 22, 10.22, &c.; 2 *p. p.* cam 17 24, ccm(e) 15.25, 19.22; *pl.* com 28.54.
Commandmentis, *sb. pl.* commandments, 25.42.
Concele, concell, consaill, consell, consylle, counsall, councill, cowu-

celle, cowsayl, *vb.* 1 *p. pr.* counsel, advise 7.21, 8.27, 9 25, 10.25, 11.25, 26.67, 29.3, 61, 30.25, 31.25.
Conclusion, *sb.* close, termination, 28.36.
Consayfe, *vb.* conceive, grasp, understand 25.31.
Consider(e), consedur, considder, considdir, consyder(e), consydre, *vb.* consider 7.13, 10.21, 11.21, 13.25, 15.36, 29.57, 30.21, 31.21.
Coveytous, *sb.* covetousness 33.55, *Conf. of ending for* covetise, OF. coveitise. Cf. *Paston Letters*, No. 582, II. 313, the unkyndnesse and covetuse that was shewed me.
Crose, *sb.* cross 25.46.
Crownnys, *sb. pl.* crowns 27.24.
Crystyn, *a.* christian 11.28.

Dai, day(e), *sb.* day 4.78, 8.24, 15.20, 21.62, 32.22.
Dare, *vb. subj.* need 34.58; ME. thar *for* tharf, OE. þearf; *from confusion with* dare, OE. dearr.
Dart, *sb.* 28.50.
Dede, *sb.* deed 4.78; *pl.* deden, dedis 2.15, 25.54.
Dedly, *a.* deadly, mortal 22.78, 23.128.
Delful, dolfull, *a.* sorrowful, doleful 1.4, 7.8, 33.28; OF. doel, duel, deol, mod. F. deuil.
Delip, *vb.* 3 *p. pr.* divides, separates 4.78.
Depairting, *sb.* separation, parting 30.8, 31.8.
Dere, *vb.* harm, injure 28.50; OE. derian.
Deth(e), deeþ, *sb.* death 5.24, 8.3, 9.30, 31, 13.3, 4, 14.2, &c.; *gen.* dethis 22.70.
Deyle, *vb. imp.* distribute 25.43.
Dignite, dignitie, dignyte, dignytie, dygnite, dygnyte, dyngnyte, *sb.* high estate or position, honour 6.2, 11.2, 12.4, 14.5, 16.4, 19.2, 20.8, 27.2, 30.2, 31.2.
Disgesily, *adv.* strangely, extraordinarily 21.42; OF. desguisié, disguised.
Do, *vb.* 34.68; 3 *p. pr.* doþe, dooþ, doith, dose 7.17, 14.2, 22.94, 25.54; *pl. p.* don 33.33; *imp.* do 26.73; *pl. p.* did 28.44; *p. pr.* doynge 23.130; *pp.* do, don 23.115, 122, 34.66.
Doluyn, *pp.* buried 23.113.
Dome, *sb.* judgement 4.76.

E 2

GLOSSARY.

Draught, draut, drawght(e), drawȝt, *sb.* drawing of a bow, bowshot 5.24, 8.3, 9.31, 13.4, 14.2. Cf. R. Brunne *Chron. Wace* (c. 1330) 862, al vnwyllnnd þat draught he drow.
Drawe, *vb.* draw 14.1; 3 *p. pr.* drawethe, drawith, drawyth(e) 5.24, 8.3, 9.31, 13.4, 20.3; 3 *p. p.* drob, drow 1.2, 4.
Dred(e), *vb imp.* dread 4.76, 23.117.
Dredfull, *a.* dreadful, terrible 28.50.
Drynkis, *sb. pl.* drinking feasts 22.86.
Duly, *adv.* duly, rightly 25.43.
Dute, *sb.* duty, dues 5.7.
Dwelle, dweylle, *vb.* dwell 22.80, 26.63; 3 *p. pr.* dwellyth 34.65.
Dye, *vb.* die 9.15; 3 *p. p.* deyd 34.78.

Earth, eird, erth, erthe, herth, *sb.* earth 1.1, &c., &c.
Empire, *sb.* 28.31.
Enclyn, *vb.* incline, be disposed, desire 27.23.
End, *vb.* 2.29.
Ende, *sb.* end 4.73, 24.6, 26.66.
Endure, *vb.* 28.45.
Ensure, *vb.* 28.46.
Entent, *sb.* intent, purpose 34.57.
Enuye, *sb.* envy 22.74.
Erþene, *a.* earthen 1.3.
Erthly, *a.* earthly 33.55, 34.70.
Est, *sb.* east, (*perh. erron. for* erth) 34.79.
Euer(e), *adv.* ever 14.35, 16.50, 18.49, 22.80, 23.130, 33.35, 36.
Euerlastynge, *a.* everlasting 23.108.
Evill, ewill, *a.* evil 30.20, 31.20.
Ewyne, *sb.* even 25.51. For oode ne for ewyne, for odd nor even, on no account whatever. Cf. even and odd, all included, without exception.
Exampul, *sb.* example 25.39.
Excludid, *pp.* excluded 22.76.

Falle, *sb.* 12.22.
Fallip, *vb* 3 *p. pr.* falls, 1.3.
Falshede, falshode, *sb.* falsehood 23.106, 110.
Falsly, *adv.* falsely 33.50.
Fane, fayne, *a.* fain 30.5, 31.5.
Fare, *vb.* go 24.12.
Fase, *sb. pl.* foes 12.28.
Fast, *adv.* 34.60.
Favtt, *vb. p. pl.* fought 25.44.

Fayr, *a.* fair 33 42; *adv.* fayre 33.50.
Fede, feden, *vb.* feed 2.14, 33.44.
Fele, *sb.*, *prob.* fell, moor 24.30; ON. fjallr.
Felow, *sb.* fellow 22.92.
Ferde, *pp.* afraid, terrified 12.24. OE. (for)fǣred.
Fere, *sb.* fear 28.52.
Festis, *sb. pl.* feasts, 22.86.
First, fyrst, *a. & adv.* 23.102, 28.31, 38, 32.14.
Flesch, *sb.* flesh 33.45.
Florische, florisshe, fflorysshe, *vb.* adorn, embellish 15.21, 17.20, 19.18, 21.63; OF. florir, floriss-.
Flowre, *sb.* flower 28.38; *pl.* flowres 34.65.
Folk, *sb.* 28.45.
Foo, *sb.* foe 22.78; *pl.* fase 12.28.
Forbere, *vb.* forbear 28.51.
Forsake, *sb. subj.* 22.81, 23.109.
Forsuthe, *int.* forsooth 12.28.
Fote, *sb.* foot 23.114; *pl.* 32.22.
Fovde, *sb.* food 25.44.
Foul(e), foulle, fovl, fowll(e), *a.* foul 5.20, 6.20, 8.22, 11.20, 22.77, 24.28, &c.
Fowle, *sb.* evil, hurt 33.39. Cf. Sowdone of Babylone (c. 1400) 199, foule shall hem this day bifalle. *NE. sense of* foul *as* trip, collision, *not found in ME.*
Frendschip, *sb.* friendship, 2.42.
Frow, *adv.* (*glossed* festine) swiftly, hastily 1.3; ON. frār, swift.
Fugure, *sb.* figure 28.47.
Ful, full(e), *adv.* fully 5.24, 9.32, 13.4, &c.
Fulfille, fulfyle, *vb.* fulfil 23.124, 25.42, 50.
Fyghtys, *vb.* 3 *p. pr.* fights, 34.60, *p. pl.* favtt 25.44.
Fynd(e), *vb.* find 12.28, 33.49; 1 *p. pr.* 25.39, 40.
Fyne, *sb.* end 27.24.

Ga, gase, *v.* go, goest 6.16, 12.27, &c.
Garnament, garnement, *sb. early form of* garment 15.28, 17.27, 21.38.
Gate, *sb.* gate 22.76.
Gatis, *sb. pl.* way 12.27.
Gay(e), *a.* 8.25, 9.23, 19.19, &c.
Gersom, *sb.* treasure, 3.61; OE. gersume.
Gett, *vb.* get 25.60; 3 *p. pr.* get hit (? *erron. for* getith, *glossed* lucratur) 2.37, getyth 34.66; 3 *p. p.* gete, gette 3.61, 10.2; *pp.* gete(n),

getyn, goten, gottin, gotyn 3.53, 5.2, 6.2, 11.2, 13.6, 19.2, 30.2, &c.

Gleterande, gleteryng(e), gletterant, *p. pr.* glittering 6.14, 8.16, 9.14, 13.18, 17.16, 20.32; *v.* Gliteringe.

Glisteryng, *p. pr.* sparkling, glittering 11.15; MLG. glistern.

Gliteringe, glitterand, glyt(t)ryng, glytteryng, *p. pr.* glittering 5.14, 12.13, 14.17, 19.14, 24.21, 30.15, 31.15; ON. glitra, to shine.

Glydderande, glyd(e)ryng, *p.pr. for* glitterande, &c. 7.18, 10.14, 27.14; *v.* Gliteringe.

Glydys, *vb.* 3 *p.pr. for* glytys, glitters 33.34; ON. glita, to shine.

Go(e), gon, goo, 3a, *vb.* go 5.15, 16, 6.15, 16, 7.19, 22.82, &c.; 2 *p. pr.* gase, goist 12.27, 22.70; 3 *p. pr.* ge(e)th, goeth, gois, go(o)th(e), gos(e), goos, gott,goyth(e), 2.13, 28, 5.14, 6.13, 14, 8.16, 9.13, 14, 11.6, 12.13, 15, 14.16, 17, 30.6, 15, 22, 32.15, 19, &c.; 3 *p. subj.* go 3.64; *imp.* go 25.47.

God, *sb. n. pr.* 7.23, 8.29, 9.27, &c.; *gen.* Goddis 23.124.

Gold(e), *sb.* 3.61, 5.14, 6.13, 14, &c.

Good, *a.* 34.57.

Goode, *sb.* property, 25.43; *pl.* goodis 23.112.

Gospel, *sb.* 25.39.

Govern, *vb.* 12.30.

Grace, *sb.* 22.70; 26.61.

Grauip, *vb.* 3 *p. pr.* buries, covers up, 3.52; OE. grafan.

Grawnte, *vb. subj.* grant 12.30.

Grene, *a.* green 3.52.

Gret(e), grit, *a.* great 21.44, 30.17, 31.12, 17, 33.52, 56, 34.80.

Grouer, *sb.* a kind of fur, 3.51; OF. gros vair, *opposed to* menu vair, minever.

Grounde, *sb.* bottom, 34.77; cf. OE. helle grund.

Groy, *sb.* grey fur, 3.51, erron. *for* grey, *or perhaps contamination of* ME. gra, gro (ON. grār) *with* grey (OE. græg). Cf. Berners *Froiss.* II. ccii. 622, furred with Myneuere and gray.

Grucche, *sb.* grudge 28.55. To strive of grucche, to strive against as a grievance.

Haf(e), *vb.* have 6.8, 20, 10.8, 20, 12.8, 20, 22.

Hallys, *sb. pl.* halls 32.5, 34.63.

Hame, *sb.* home 30.7, 31.7.

Hande, *sb.* 24.24.

Happe, *vb.* wrap 15.29.

Hard(e), herd, *a.* hard 6.8, 11.8, 12, 30.8, 31.8, &c.

Hart, herte, *sb.* heart 25.46, 33.53.

Hartily, hertili, hertly, *adv.* heartily 15.40, 18 39, 21.54.

Haste, *sb.* 25.53.

Hate, *sb.* 22.74.

Hate, *vb.* hate; 3 *p.pr.* hatid 2.26; *pp.* hated, hatid, hatyd(e) 5.23, 8.2, 9.30, 13.3, 14.1, 16.2, 17.26, 20.2.

Hauntist, *vb.* 2 *p. pr.* practisest habitually 22.74.

Haue, have, haf(e), *vb.* have 5.8, 20, 6.8, 20, 8.10, 22, 10.8, 20, &c.; 1 *p. pr.* haue 28.44; 2 *p. pr.* hase, hast(e), 12.25, 28, 13.29, &c.; 3 *p. pr.* has(e), hath(e) 1.1, 2.27, 5.2, 3, 12.1, 11, &c.; hes 30.2, 11, 31.2, 11; *pr. pl.* haue 29.61; *imp.* haue 28.52; 3 *p. subj.* haue 34.65; 3 *p.p.* had(e), heuede 1.4, 29.3, 34.72.

Hede, *sb.* head 25.48.

Hede, *sb.* heed 24.5.

Heere, here, *adv.* 16.48, 28.40, 45.

Heghe, hey, *v.* hi3 6.4, 11.4.

Hel(e), hell, *vb.* hell 25.40, 58, 34.77.

Helpe, *sb.* 26.72.

Helpyne, *vb.* 3 *pl. pr.* help 25.52.

Hend, *a.* gracious 4.75.

Hennys, *adv.* hence 22.82.

Herd, herte, hertili, *v.* Hard, Hart, Hartily.

Hete, *sb.* heat 28.43.

Heuen(e), heuyn, heyuyn(e), heywyn, *sb.* heaven 15.43, 19.24, 25 40, 52, 26.63, 34.82, &c.

Heuy, *a.* heavy 9.8.

Hicht, *sb.* height 30.4, 31.4.

Hide, hyde, *vb.* 15.29, 17.28, 21.39.

Hider, hidir, hyder, *adv.* hither 15.25, 17.24, 19.22.

Hidiose, hidous, *a.* hideous 15.31, 17.30.

Hi3, hihe, heghe, hey, hy(e), hy3, hygh(e), *a. & adv.* high 5.4, 6.4, 7.4, 8.4, 9.3, 10.4, 11.4, 11, 12.2, 13.8, 14 7, 16. 6, 51, 19.4, 22.100; hiere (higher) 20.12.

Hille, hylle, *sb.* hill 14.36, 16.51, 18.50, 23.132.

Hold, *vb.*; 3 *p. pr.* holdys 32.16; *pp.* hold 28.30.

Hold, *a.* faithful 3.63.

Holy, *a.* holy 23.132.

GLOSSARY.

Hom(e), hoom, whom(e), *sb.* home 5.7, 6.7, 11.7, 16.9, 24.9, &c.; *v.* hame.
Honger, *sb.* hunger 34.72.
Honour, *sb.* 27.22.
Houe, hove, how(e) *conj.* how 5.4, 6, 6.4, 6, 7.4, 6, &c., &c.
Hows, *sb.* house 32.26.
Hundred, *num.* 2.18.

Idiʒte, *pp.* placed, set 2.38.
Ilich, alike 1.5.
Ille, ylle, *a. & adv.* ill 14.33, 16.48, 18.47, 23.122.
Ilor, *pp.* lost 2.42; *v.* Loste.
Imeten, *pp.* measured 3.54.
Inow(e), ynoh, enough 1.2, 4, 32.18.
Iustly, *adv.* justly 5.16.
Iustyse, *sb.* justice, judge, 22.100.

Karful, *a.* grievous, sad, full of care, 26 64.
King, kyng(e), *sb.* 2.39, 5.5, 7.5, 8.7, 9.5, &c.
Klyng, *v.* clinge.
Kniʒt, knyght, *sb.* knight 2.39, 19.24.
Know, *vb.* 27.23; 3 *p. pr.* knowethe 9.21.
Knyʒthode, *sb.* 28.38.

Labour, *vb.* 23.103.
Ladis, *sb.* Lady's 26.72.
Lang, long, *a.* 3.50, 64; *adv.* 28.45, 33.40.
Lappe, *vb.* wrap 21.39.
Last(e), *a.* 4.73, 12.23, 32.22; at þe last 33.39, 34.62.
Late, lete, lett, *vb. imp.* let 14.34, 16.49, 18.48, 23.127, 25.51.
Lay, *vb.*; 3 *p. pr.* layes 32.3; 3 *p. p.* leyd(e) 1.3, 27.24; *pp.* layd(e) 33.44, 54, 34.64.
Lede, *vb. subj.* lead 25.58, 34.82.
Leinþ, *sb.* length 3.54.
Leniþ, *vb.* 3 *p. pr.* rewards 4.78. OE. lēanian.
Lent(e), y-lent, *pp.* lent, granted 15.29, 17.28, 21.40. OE. lǣnan.
Lest(e), *conj.* 4.76, 25.58.
Leve, lyffe, *vb.* live 19.24, 28.41, 33.35; 2 *p. pr.* leuyst, leuuyst 25.50, 26.62; 3 *p. pr.* lyueth 23.105; *imp.* lyffe 19.23; 3 *p. p.* levyd 34.57.
Lewe, *vb. imp.* leave 19.29.
Lif(e), liif, lyf(e), lyffe, *sb.* life 2.15, 5.23, 8.2, 9.29, 13.3, 14.1, 16.1, 20.1.

Liʒt, lyt, *vb.* alight, descend; 3 *p. p.* lytyd 34.75; *pp.* liʒt 2.40.
Like, lyk(e), *conj.* like 5.15, 6 15, 7.19, 8.17, 9.15, &c.
List, lyst, *vb.* desire 28.47; 3 *p. p.* liste 27.23.
Liuerei, *sb.* livery, 3.52.
Logege, *vb.* lodge 25.58.
Loke, *vb. imp.* look 25.51.
Lond, *sb.* land 4.73.
Lord(e), *nom. pr.* 14.33, 16.48, 18.47, 23.125, 25.45.
Loste, *vb. p. pl.* lost 28.28.; *v.* Ilor.
Loth, *a.* loth, unwilling 33.54.
Loue, *sb.* love 23.119, 25.45, 32.13.
Loue, love, *vb.* love; 2 *p. pr.* louyst 22.77; 3 *p. pr.* loues, -is, -ys, 9.17, 10.17, 24.25, 33.29; loueth, -yth, loveth, -yth(e), loweth 5.17, 8.19, 11.17, 17.31, 27.17; lu(i)ffis 6.17, 12.17, 30.17, 31.17; *pp.* loued, louyd(e) 5.23, 8.2, 9.29, 13.3, &c.
Lowʒ, *adv.* low 2.40.
Lust, *sb.* desire 22.83.
Lutil, *adv.* little 8.50.
Ly, *vb.* lie 32.26; 3 *p. pr.* lyis 24.30; *pl. pr.* lye 26.32.
Lyffe, lyueth, *v.* Leve.
Lykyng, *p. pr.* pleasing, desirable 32.23.

Mai, may(e), *vb. pr. sg.* may 1.2, 5.4, 6.4, &c., &c.; *pl.* 28.45; 2 *p. pr.* moue 25.56; 3 *p. p.* myght, myth 7.4, 24, 9.3, 27.4.
Maistri, *sb.* mastery, lordship 2.37; *pl.* maistres 12.26.
Make, *vb. subj.* 15.22, 19.19, 21.66, 33.36; 2 *p. pr.* mase 12.26; 3 *p. pr.* maketh, -ith, -yth(e) 5.24, 8.3, 9.32, 14.2, 16.2; 2 *p. p.* madist, -yst 14.33, 16.48, 18.47; 3 *p. p.* mad(e) 26.69, 32.11, 34.69; maid 30.27, 31.27; *p. pr.* makyng 22.90; *pp.* made 20.14, 22.87, 23.101, 27.24; maked, -id, 1.5, 15.24, 17.23, 19.21.
Man, mon, *sb.* man 4.71, 77, 5.17, 24, &c.
Maner, *sb.* 22.96; any maner wise, any kind of way.
Many, *a.* 11.12, 12.28, 34.76.
Mast, *sb.* 34.59.
Mede, *sb.* meed, reward 4.77, 33.43; *pl.* meden 2.16.
Mekyl, *a.* much 33.49; *v.* Moche, myche.
Mercy, *sb.* 25.50.
Merwel, *sb.* marvel 24.25.

GLOSSARY. 55

Miȝte, *sb.* power, might 2.37.
Miseislich, *adv.* uncomfortably 3.54.
Moche, myche, *a.* much 4.77; *adv.* 15.32; *v.* Mekyl.
Moder, *sb.* mother 3.62.
Mold, *sb.* mould, pattern, 3.62; OFr. modle.
Mold(e), moolde, moulde, mowld e), *sb.* mould, earth 5.13, 7.17, 9.13, 10.13, 11.13, 17.15, &c.
Molys, *sb. pl.* moles 33.33.
Mone, *sb.* moan 22.90.
More, *adv.* 6.15, 28.34, 33.35, 36; moo 22.80; *a.* 28.40.
Most(e), moost, *adv.* 5.23, 8.2, 14.1, &c.
Moue, *vb.* 2 *p. pr.* may 25.56; see Mai.
Muntid, *vb.* 3 *p. pr.* 2.16 (glossed metitur) measures, appoints; OE. myntan, to intend, propose, hint.
Mynd(e), *sb.* 25.38, 33.36.
Myrth(e), *sb.* mirth, joy 26.64, 66.
Myscheue, *vb. subj.* come to grief, meet with misfortune 16.49, 18.48; O.F. meschever.
Myschyffe, *sb.* misfortune, evil plight 14.34.
Mysdon, misdone 34.66.
Myse, *vb.* miss 26.64.
Mysgete, *p.* misgotten 23.112.
Mysplese, *vb.* displease 15.43, 17.42, 21.60.

Naked, nakid, -it, -yd(e), -yt, *a.* naked 5.24, 7.14, 8.24, 15.37, 25.32, &c.
Namyd, *vb.* 3 *p. p.* named 34.69.
Nawte, *pr., v.* Nocht, noght.
Nede, *sb.* need 34.80.
Neuer(e), neuyr(e), never, nevyr, *adv.* never 5.15, 7.19, 8.17, 15.22, 17.21, 19.15, 34.58, &c.
Niȝt, nyȝt, nyght, nyht, *sb.* night 4.78, 15.20, 17.19, 19.17, 21.62.
Nim, *vb.* take 1.2, OE. niman.
Noblenes, *sb.* high estate, nobility 28.35.
Nobley, nobylay, *sb.* noble estate or condition 10.2, 32.2.
Nobul, *a.* noble 5.2.
Nocht, noght(e), nogth, noht, nouȝt, nought(e), nowght, nawte, *pr.* nought 5.2, 6.2, 7.2, 9.4, &c.
Non(e), *pr.* none 22.92, 28.27, 34.61.
Nor, *conj.* than 30.16, 31.16.
Nother, *conj.* neither 25.60.
Nothing(e), nothyng(e), *pr.* nothing 5.6, 9.6, 24.8, 31.6.

Now(e), *adv.* 28.41, 31.10, 32.3.
Old(e), *a.* old 28.41, 34.74.
Onkynde, *a.* unkind, unnatural 33.47.
Oode, *sb.* odd 25 51, for oode ne for ewyne, for odd nor even, on no account.
Opon, *prep. var. of* upon 12.1, 2, &c.
Or, *adv.* before 23.113, 28.50; OE. ǣr.
Ordande, *vb.* 3 *p. p.* ordained 12.29.
Oribyll, *a.* horrible 21.52.
Othe, *sb.* oath 33.52.
Oper, *a.* other 1.2.
Other, owther, owþir, *conj.* either, or 6.18, 11.18, 30.18, 31.18.
Our(e)s, ouris, -us, -ys, owres, -is, -ys, owrris, houris, *pron.* ours 5.10, 6.10, 7.10, 8.12, 9.10, &c , &c.
Owris, ? ours 24.23.

Pale, *a.* 28.32.
Palfrei, palfreye, *sb.* palfrey 3.49, 32.20.
Paradys, *sb.* Paradise 34.70.
Parting, partyng(e), parttynge, *sb.* parting, leave-taking, 5.8, 6.8, 14.11, 24.10, &c.
Pas(e), passe, *vb.* pass 8.26, 9.24, 10.24, 25.34, &c.
Payne, *sb.* pain 23.108, *pl.* paynes, peynes, peynys 14.33, 16.48, 18.47, 23.126.
Paynt(e), peynte, *vb.* paint 15.21, 17.20, 19.18, 21.63.
Pepul, *sb.* people, 25.44.
Perische, *vb. subj.* perish 22.99.
Petous, petus, *a.* 10.8, 16.10, 20.20; *v.* Piteuous.
Petrus, *a.* ? piteous 5.8.
Piteuous, pyteous, pytous, pytyus, *a.* piteous 8.10, 13.12, 14.11, 19.8.
Place, *sb.* 25.48, 26.62.
Playn, *a.* plain 28 47.
Plese, *vb.*, please 22.95.
Plowe, *sb.* plough 32.15.
Poor(e), por(e), pure, *a.* poor 7.16, 10.24, 11.24, 15.25, 39, 30.24, &c.
Pore, *sb.* the poor, 1.6.
Portratowre, *sb.* portraiture 28.48.
Praie, pray(e), preye, *vb.* 8.29, 10.27, &c., *imp.* 13.31, 15.46, 18.45, 29.63; 1 *p. pr.* 9.27; *pr. pl.* 7.23.
Prankys, *vb.* 3 *p. pr.* to show oneself off, strut, parade 32.20; MDu. pronken.
Pride, *sb.* 33.53.
Prode, proud, prowde, prowt, prude, *a.* proud 7.15, 15.24, 17.23, 19.21, 25.33.

GLOSSARY.

Prykys, *vb.* 3 *p. pr.* to spur one's horse 32.20.
Punsched, *pp.* punished 23.108.
Purvey, purway, *vb.* make provision 28.52; provide, furnish 26.62.
Pyne, *sb.* pain 25.59.

Quene, *sb.* queen 3.49.
Queynt(e), *a.* ingenious, elaborate, fine 15.22, 17.21, 19.19.
Queytith, *vb.* 3 *p. pr.* requiteth 22.93.
Quhen, quhone, *adv.* 30.7, 11, 19, 31.7, 11, 19; *v.* Whan(ne), when(ne).
Quhill, quhy, 30.23, 26, 31.23, 26; *v.* While, Whi.

Race, *vb.* to tear away, snatch 22.72; OF. racher, -ier, *from* arrachier.
Ragged, raggid, *a.* 15.30, 17.29, 21.42.
Rakid, *pp.* raked, covered, buried 15.26, 17.25; ON. raka to scrape, rake, cf. Ch. Monkes T. 143 in hoote coles he hath hym seluen raked.
Rank, *a.* proud, haughty 15.27, 17.26.
Rather(e), rathar, rathyr, *adv.* 5.16, 6.16, 7.20, &c.
Recke, *vb.* reck, care, heed 34.58.
Rede, *vb.* read 25.47; guide, direct 33.46.
Rekenyng(e), rikenynge, *sb.* account 15.42, 18.41, 21.58.
Rekyn, *vb. subj.* reckon, take count of 28.37.
Renown, *sb.* 28.33.
Rent, to-rent, *pp.* rent, torn 15.30, 17.29, 21.42, 25.45.
Rent(e), *sb.* revenue, income, tribute 7.7, 9.7, 10.7, &c.; *pl.* rentes, -is, -ys, 6.7, 8.9, 11.7, &c.
Repente, *vb. imp.* 23.121.
Resoune, *sb.* reason 23.118.
Reste, *vb.* rest 25.48.
Restore, *vb. imp.* 23.111.
Rewful, rewfulle, *a.* rueful 15.35, 17.34.
Riche, rych, *sb.* rich 1.6, 25.40.
Right, *sb.* righteousness, good 2.41.
Right, riht, ryght, *a.* 34.82; *adv.* 5.20, 21.58, 33.46.
Risynge, *sb.* uprising, resurrection 18.40, 21.56.
Rode, roode, *sb.* rood 25.45, 34.78.
Rof, *sb.* roof 2.17, 32.26.
Ros, *vb.* 3 *p. p.* rose 34.79.

Ruli, ruly, *a. or adv.* rueful(ly) 15.30, 17.29, OE. hrēowlīc.
Ryches, *sb. pl.* riches 25.38.
Rydys, *vb.* 3 *p. pr.* rides 33.42.

Sake, *sb.* 33.38.
Salle, *sb.* hall, palace, court 12.24.
Same, *a.* 32.11.
Saule, *sb.* soul 12.32; *v.* Soule.
Save, sawe, *vb.* save 34.77; 3 *p. pr.* sauyd 34.76.
Say, *vb.* 12.21; 3 *p. pr.* sais(e), sase 6.10, 12.10, saith(e), sayth(e) 5.10, 8.12, 20.27, 22.91; sayis, says 10.10, 30.10, 31.10, seiþ, seyth, seth 7.10, 11.10, 14.13, &c.
Schal, shall, *vb.* shall; 2 *p. pr.* schalt, 2.29; 3 *p. pr.* sal(e), sc(h)al, schall(e), shall(e) 5.8, 12, 6.8, 16, 7.6, 20, &c.; *pl.* schullen 2.18; 2 *p. p.* schuldist 22.80; 3 *p. p.* scholde, schould(e), schuld(e), shuld, sold, sulde 6.15, 9.15, 23, 10.23, &c.
Scharp(e), sharp(e), *a.* sharp 5.12, 6.12, 8.14, 17.14, 30.12, &c.
Sched, *vb.* 3 *p. p.* shed 25.46.
Schend, *vb. subj.* shame, disgrace 4.76; *pp.* schent 33.55.
Schene, *a.* bright, beautiful 3.51.
Schouris, -ys, schowres, -is, -ys, shour(e)s, showres, -is, *sb. pl.* 5.12, 7.12, 8.14, &c., &c.; scowrrys 6.12, schorrys 24.16.
Schroud, schrud, shroude, shrowde, *sb.* clothing 3.51, 15.25, 17.24, 19.22.
Scowrrys, *sb. pl.* 6.12, showers; (*or perh.* stourrys, battles, tumults, OF. estor, estour).
Secatours, *sb. pl.* executors 24.24, ME. *also* secetour, sectour.
Securlye, *adv.* certainly, surely, 26.66.
Sely, *a.* blessed 12.24; simple 32.24.
Sen, syn, *conj.* since 8.26, 25.34, 30.24.
Seruyse, *sb.* service 22.94.
Set, *vb.* 3 *p. pr.* sattys 32.4; *pp.* set(e), sett(e), ysette 5.3, 6.3, 7.3, &c.
Seth(e), sethen, sith, syth, *conj.* since 9.24, 10.24, 11.24, 29.60, 32.12.
Seven, *nu.* 32.22.
Seynt Powlis, 28.48 St. Paul's.
Shewith, *vb.* 3 *p. pr.* shews 28.49.
Short, *a.* 28.36.
Shyne, *vb.* shine 27.22.
Sin, synne, *sb.* sin, 4.76, 23.115.
Skin, *sb.* 2.18.

GLOSSARY. 57

Skyle, *sb.* reason 25.41.
Slogh, *sb.* slough, skin, covering, 32.17, 33.40.
Smarte, *sb.* smart, pain 24.17.
Smele, *vb.* smell 24.29.
Socowre, *sb.* succour 28.40.
Soffyre, sofur, *vb.* 10.12, 24.16; *v.* Suffer.
Solde, *pp.* sold 34.73.
Sone, *adv.* soon 33.48; sonar, sone(a)r 27.16, 30.16, 31.16.
Sore, *a.* sore, grievous 23.104; *adv.* 15.33, 23.116.
Sorow(e), *sb.* sorrow 22.84, 34.81.
Soule, sowle, *sb.* soul 3.63, 33.38; *v.* Saule.
Space, *sb.* space of time, respite 26.63.
Sped(e), *vb.* speed 24.6, 34.81.
Spille, spylle, *vb.* perish, be destroyed 14.34, 16.49, 18.48, 23.128.
Starte, *sb.* a sudden movement 24.18. Thi lyfe ys but a starte, but for a moment.
Stede, *sb.* steed 33.42.
Stelis, *vb.* 3 *p. pr.* steals 32.17.
Steyuyne, *sb.* voice 25.49; OE. stefn.
Stie, stye, *vb.* ascend, mount 14.36, 16.51, 18.50, 23.132; OE. stīgan.
Stille, *adv.* silently 23.126.
Stink, stynk(e), *sb.* stink 6.20, 8.22, 30.20, 31.20, &c.
Stounde, *sb.* hour 34.75; OE. stund.
Stourrys, *sb. pl.* conflicts 6.12; OF. estor, (*probably* Scourrys; *v.* Schouris).
Stoute, stowte, *a.* bold, proud 8.25, 9.23, 15.38, &c.; cf. OF. estout.
Streinþ, *sb.* force, violence 3.53.
Streite, streyt, *a.* close, exact 15.42, 17.41, 21.58.
Streytly, *adv.* closely 28.39.
Strive, stryue, *vb.* 22 72, 28.55.
Stronge, *a.* strong 34.59.
Styke, *sb.* 5.20, *erron. for* stynke.
Suffer, -ir(e), -yr(e), suffre, soffyre, sofur, *vb.* suffer 5.12, 6.12, 7.12, 8.14, 9.12, 10.12, 11.12, 24.16, &c.; 2 *p. p.* sufferdyst, suffredist, suffridist 14.32, 16.48, 18.47, 23.126.
Superflue, *a.* superfluous 15.33.
Sweet(e), sweit, swet(e), swett, *vb.* sweat 5.18, 6.18, 11.18, 15.33, 21.48, 31.18, &c.; 3 *p. pr.* swetys 10.18.
Swerys, *vb.* 3 *p. pr.* swears 33.52.
Swink(e), swynk(e), *vb.* toil, labour, *ref. as for* sweet(e) *supra.* 3 *p. pr.* swynkes 10.18.

Swynkynge, labour, exertion 23.104.
Symple, *a.* simple 25.34.
Syttythe, *vb.* 3 *p. pr.* sits 9.11.

Take, *vb.* 33.37, 39; *imp.* 24.5, 25.49; 3 *p. pr.* takys 32.2; 2 *p. p.* tokist 23.125; 3 *p. p.* toc, toke 1.1, 34.81; *pp.* taken 12.31.
Tent, *sb.* heed, attention 25.49.
Teriþ, *vb.* 3 *p. pr.* tears 2.27.
Than(ne), then(ne), *adv.* then, 1.2, 2.18, 5.12, 11.8, &c., &c.
That, *pron. and conj.* 2.30, 3.51, 6.17, &c.; *pl.* þose 7.10.
Thenk, think(e), thynk, *vb.* think 15.40, 17.39, 21.46; *imp.* 4.72, 12.26, 28.42; 1 *p. pr.* 8.19, 27.17, 30.17, 31.17; me think(e), thynke, thynkes 5.17, 6.17, 9.17, 10.17, &c.; 3 *p. pr.* þenkiþ, thenkys 10.6, 14.9; think's, thynketh(e), -ith, -yth(e), -is, -ys(e), thyngkethe, thyngkys 5.6, 6.6, 8.8, 9.4, 11.6, 13.10, 16.8, 19.6, &c.; *p. pr.* thynkyng 20.16.
This, thys, *pron.* 5.10, 6.10, &c.; *pl.* these 13.14; þir 30.10.
Thocht, thoght(e), thought(e), þouȝt(e), thouthe, thowght(e), thowht, thowth, *sb.* thought 5.3, 6.3, 7.3, 22, 8.5, 28, 9.2, 26, 10.3, 26, 11.3, 26, 12.1, &c., &c.
Thynkynge, *sb.* thought, consideration, 21.54.
Thorow, *prep.* through, 26.72.
þre, *nu.* three 2.42.
þroh, prouȝ, *sb.* coffin, 1.3, 2.42; O.E. þrūh.
Thouh, þouw, *conj.* though 3.50, 21.33.
Till, *prep.* to, 30.4, 31.4.
Toght, *adv.* 32.16, *prob. erron. for* togh, tough; *rimes* plowe, slogh, inowe.
Torn(e), turn(e), *vb.* turn 7.22, 8.28, 9.26, 10.26, 11.26, &c., &c.
Tour(e)s, -is, -ys, towres, -is, -ys, towrrys, *sb.* towers 3.65, 5.9, 6.9, 7.9, 9.9, 10.9, &c., &c.
Toward, *prep.* 2.14.
Trauayles, traue(i)list, traueylist, *vb.* 2 *p. pr.* labourest 15.20, 17.19, 19.17, 21.62.
Trede, *vb.* tread; *pp.* ytrede 23.114.
Trewth, trowthe, *sb.* truth 23.104, 28.47.
Tristyn, *vb.* trust 22.95; *imp.* trust 24.24.
Turment, *sb.* torment 15.31, 17.30, 21.44.

GLOSSARY.

Tyllys, *vb.* 3 *p. pr.* tills the ground, 32.15.
Tyme, *sb.* time, 12.21.

Unclade, *a.* 25.35.
Undeuout, *a.* undevout, 15.27.
Unresonably, *adv.* unreasonably, 21.48.
Unreydy, *a.* unready 25.56.
Unsiker, *a.* uncertain, 28.43.
Upon, uppon, vp(p)on, vpoun, *prep.* 5.3, 4, 5, &c., 8.5, 7, &c.; *v* Apon, Opon, Ypon.
Upsodown, *adv.* upside-down 28.35, *from* up swa down.

Vayn, in vayn, in vain 28.55.
Vede, *sb.*, *for* weed—dress, apparel 33.41.
Verrid, *vb.* 3 *p. pr.* warreth 2.26.

Walk, *vb.*; 3 *p. p.* walkyd 34.71; *p. pr.* walkand 33.41.
Wan, *a.* 28.32.
Wan, *vb.* 28.29; *v.* Win.
Wanton, wantowne, *a.* 15.21, 17.20, 19.18, 21.64.
Wantyng(e), *p. pr.* lacking 17.27, 21.38.
Wars, *a.* worse 24.30.
Waxin, -yne, *pp.* waxen, grown 9.1, 32.1.
Waye, wei, wey(e), *sb.* way 3.50, 25.56, 32.19, 34.82.
Weden, *sb. pl.* weeds, apparel 2.13.
Wel(le), *adv.* well 4.75, 24.6.
Welth, *sb.* wealth, 27.13, 34.65.
Wend(e), *vb.* wend, go 2.30, 4.74, 25.56, 30.24, 31.24; *pr. pl.* wendiþ 2.41; 3 *p. p* went 34.58.
Wene, *vb.* 1 *pl. pr.* think, expect, ween 3.50.
Weriþ, *vb. pr. pl.* wear 3.51.
Werkis, werkys, *sb. pl.* works 25.50, 52.
Whan(ne), when(ne), quhen, quhene, *adv.* when 1.1, 2.17, 5.11, &c., &c.
Whar-of, whereof 4.74.
Whi, why, quhy, *conj.* 2.26, 5.17, 6.18, 8.19, &c.
While, whill, quhill, whyl(e), whyles, *conj.* while 7.22, 8.28, 9.26, 13.30, &c.; the whyle þat 10.26, 11.26.
Whoder, *adv.* whither 4.74.
Wickidli, wickydly, wikkidly, wikyd, wyckydly, wykedly, wy(k)kydly, wykydely, wvkytly, *adv.* wickedly 7.21, 8.27, 10.25, 13.29, 15.44, 18.43, 26.67, 29.3, 61.

Will, wyl, wyll(e), wol(e), *vb.* 3 *p. pr.* 5.18, 12.18, 13.22, 15.33, 17.32, 21.48, &c.; 3 *p. p. & p. pl.* wold(e) 5.5, 16, 6.5, 16, 7.5, 20, &c., &c.; wald 30.5, 31.16.
Wille, wylle, *sb.* will 14.35, 16.50, 18.49, 23.130.
Win, *vb.* to win; 3 *p. pr.* wins 31.9, wynneth(e), -yth(e), -es, -is, -ys, 5.9, 6.9, 7.9, 8.9, &c., &c.; 2 *p. p.* wonne 2.30; 3 *p. p.* wan 28.29; *pp.* iwonne 1.1.
Wise, *sb.* manner, fashion, guise, 22.96.
Wisely, *adv.* 28.52.
Within, -inne, -yn, -ynne, *adv.* 5.19, &c., &c.
Withowttyn, wittovte, *prep.* without 25.48, 26.66.
Witte, *sb.* wit, intelligence 23.118.
Wo, woo, *sb.* woe 12.32, 22.84.
Woh, wow, *sb.* evil 1.1; *pl.* wowȝ 2.41. OE. wōh, wōȝ-, crooked, evil.
Wol(e) 15.33, 17.32, 21.48; *v.* Will.
Woman, *sb.* 32.13.
Wonder, -ir(e), wondre, wondur, wondyr, woundyr, *sb.* wonder 5.17, 6.17, 8.19, 9.17, 10.17, &c., &c.
Wonderfull, wondirfullie, *adv.* wonderfully 30.1, 31.1.
Wonderly, wondirlie, -ly, wondurly, wondyrly, wounderly, woundyrely, *adv.* wondrously 5.1, 6.1, 7.1, 8.4, 10.1, 11.1, 12.3, 13.5, 14.4, 16.3, 19.1, 20.6, 24.1, 30.25, 31.25.
Worching(e), -ynge, *p. pr.* working 14.35, 16.50, 18.49.
World, *sb.* 28.29.
Worldly, *adv.* 27.1, *perh. erron. for* wonderly.
Wormes, -ys, *sb. pl.* 2.14, 32.25, 33.44, 45, 46.
Wor-schyp, -ship, *sb.* 7.2, 12.25.
Worthy, *a.* 28.25; 30; *sb. pl.* worthyes 27.21.
Worthynes, *sb.* worthiness, honour, 28.40.
Wote, wottis, *vb.* 3 *p. pr.* knows 24.12, 33.46; 3 *p. p.* wyste 34.67.
Wounde, *sb.* wound 34.76, 78.
Wrecchid(e), wreched, -yd, *a.* wretched 15.20, 24, 28, 17.19, 23, 19.17, 21.
Wrikkend, *p. pr.* moving, walking 2.13; Dan. vrikke, Du. wrikken.
Wrocht, wroght(e), wroht, wroth, wrought(e), wrouȝt(e), wrouhte,

wrout(h)e, wrowght(e), *pp.* wrought, made 5.1, 6.1, 7.1, 23, 8.1, 27, 29, 9.1, 25, 27, &c., &c.
Wroten, *vb.* to root, turn up with the snout 2.18; 3 *p. pr.* wrotys 33.33; O.E. wrotian.
Wroth, *a.* 33.48, 51; (7.1, spelling of wroht, *v.* Wrocht, wroght).
Wryttyne, written 25.39.
Wyn, *sb.* joy, pleasure 32.25.
Wynde, *sb.* wind 33.48.
Wynde, *vb.* to wind 32.24.
Wyne, *sb.* wine 25.60.

Wyste, 34.67; *v.* Wote.

Ya, *int.* yea, verily 12.7, 11, 15.
Yelde, yeelde, ȝeelde, *vb.* yield, render, pay 15.42, 18.41, 21.58; 3 *p. pr.* yeldis 33.56.
Yeȝt, yet, ȝet, yit, ȝit(t), ȝyt(e), *adv.* yet 6.16, 7.20, 8.18, 9.12, 16, &c.
Yong, *a.* young, 28.41.
Ypon, *prep.* var. of upon 11.3.

ȝefe, ȝeyf, *vb. imp.* give 24.24, 26.61.
ȝere, *sb. pl.* years 34.74.

ADDENDA

(from the text in the Appendix).

Afrәte, *pp.* devoured, eaten 42.3.
Agrise, *vb.* tremble, quake 44.28.
Alas, *int.* 43.17.
Alete, *vb.* to let go, forsake 42.3.
Aryse, *vb.* arise 44.25.
Assise, *sb.* the Judgement 44.26.
Awelden, *vb.* wield, rule 42.9.

Belden, *vb.* build up 43.12.
Bi-holden, *vb.* keep, retain 42.10.
Byheste, *sb.* promise 45.30.
Byhet, *vb.* 3 *p. pr.* promises 45.31.

Cheste, *sb.* strife, dispute 45.29; OE. cēast, *older* cēas, L. causa.
Coueytise, *sb.* covetousness 42.6.
Crieþ, *vb.* 3 *p. pr.* cries 42.8.

Dedliche, *a.* deadly 43.14.

Elden, *vb.* to grow old 43.11.
Endinge, *sb.* 44.21.
Eorthe, *sb.* earth 42.1, &c.

Foelle, *vb. subj.* ? fall 43.20.
Forȝete, *pp.* forgotten 42.4.
Furloren, *pp.* lost 45.35.

Grimliche, *adv.* terribly 44.28.
Guo, *vb.* go 43.15.
Gynneþ, *vb.* 3 *p. pr.* begins 43.15.

Haueþ, *vb.* 3 *p. pr.* has 43.13.
Helle-feste, *sb.* Hell-fortress 45.32.
Hyeþ, *vb.* 3 *p. pr.* hastens 42.7.

Iboren, *pp.* born 45.33.
Ibouȝt, *pp.* redeemed 43.19.
Icoren, *pp. a.* chosen ones 45.35.

Igete, *pp.* got 42.1.
Ignawe, *pp.* devoured 44.23.
Ihere, *vb.* hear 44.26.
Iknawe, *vb.* know 44.24.
Iseoþ, *vb.* 3 *p. pr.* sees 43.14, 44.21.
Islawe, *pp.* slain 44.22.
Iuynt, *vb.* 3 *p. pr.* joins 42.9.
Iworthe, *vb.* become 43.16.

Lәre, *vb.* teach 44.27.
Leste, *vb.* last 45.31.
Louerd, *sb.* Lord 45.33.
Luþer, *a.* wicked 42.9.

Mychfulliche, *adv.* greatly, at so great cost 43.19.

Netfulliche, *adv.* of necessity 44.25.

Of-souȝt, *pp.* attacked 43.18.

Prude, *sb.* pride 42.5.

Seluen, *pron.* self 44.24.
Styeþ, *vb.* 3 *p. pr.* ascends, mounts up 42.5.
Sullen, *vb.* 1 *pl. pr.* shall 43.16.

Þilke, *pron.* that same 44.26.
Totoren, *pp.* torn, rent 45.34.

Wan(ne), were, when, where 42.5, 44.25, 45.30, 32.
Wise, *vb.* guide, direct 44.27.
Wrong, *sb.* 42.1.
Wryeþ, *vb.* 3 *p. pr.* turns, inclines 42.6.
Wyte, *vb. imp.* guard, keep 45.35.

The manufacturer's authorised representative in the EU for product safety is Oxford University Press España S.A. of El Parque Empresarial San Fernando de Henares, Avenida de Castilla, 2 - 28830 Madrid (www.oup.es/en or product.safety@oup.com). OUP España S.A. also acts as importer into Spain of products made by the manufacturer.
Printed and bound by CPI Group (UK) Ltd, Croydon, CR0 4YY

20/03/2026

02075339-0008